MIX-A-MEAL COOKBOOK

Mixes & Recipes

Deanna Bean & Lorna Shute

Mix-A-Meal Company
Orem, Utah 84097-1662

Printed in the United States of America

Graphic Design by Roselie Graphics
Original Art Work by WendyJo Originals

If you have any questions or comments concerning this book, please write:
Mix-A-Meal Company
PO Box 971662
Orem, UT 84097-1662

ISBN 0-9708697-0-3 (paperbound)

Making dry mixes at home is a brand new idea!
A cooking breakthrough!
It saves grocery money and time!

FUN
Meals and Treats

Made the EASY WAY
with
Homemade DRY Mixes

MIX-A-MEAL gives you the convenience of
store bought mixes
at a fraction of the cost
and they taste better!

CONTENTS

INTRODUCTION
Page 4

GIFT IDEAS
Page 8

BASIC MIXES

SAUCES AND SPICE MIXES

INSTANT MEALS

EASY FUN DESSERT MIXES

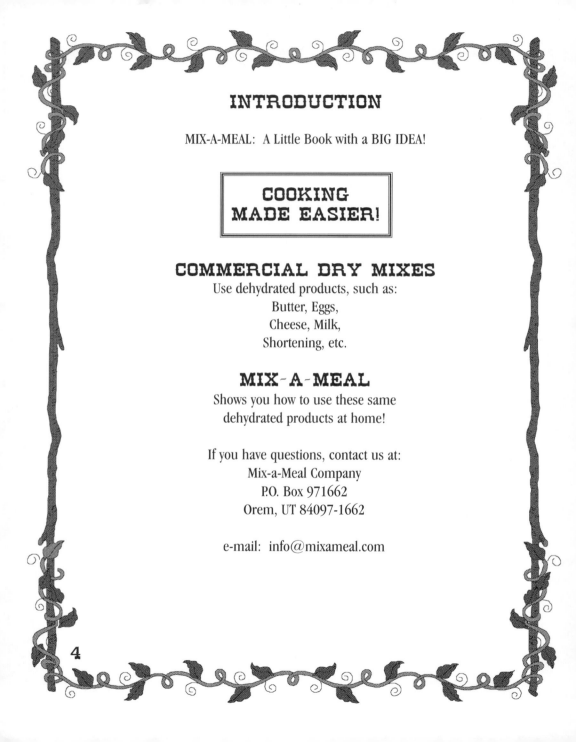

INTRODUCTION

MIX-A-MEAL: A Little Book with a BIG IDEA!

COOKING
MADE EASIER!

COMMERCIAL DRY MIXES
Use dehydrated products, such as:
Butter, Eggs,
Cheese, Milk,
Shortening, etc.

MIX-A-MEAL
Shows you how to use these same
dehydrated products at home!

If you have questions, contact us at:
Mix-a-Meal Company
P.O. Box 971662
Orem, UT 84097-1662

e-mail: info@mixameal.com

With Mix-A-Meal you will:

- Save up to 90% of the cost of commercial mixes by making your own delicious and tasty mixes!

- Spend less time in the kitchen and enjoy that good old-fashioned taste.

- Lower the preservative content in your foods.

- Adjust mixes as necessary to fit special dietary needs.

- Make a shelf-stable mix for traveling, camping trips or unexpected company.

- Enjoy no-nonsense cleanup. Just add water or a few simple ingredients.

- Give a fun and useful homemade gift for any occasion.

> Sometimes trying a new way of doing things is threatening to our "kitchen comfort zone!" This new idea, however, is so fast and easy, you'll wonder how you ever got along without it!

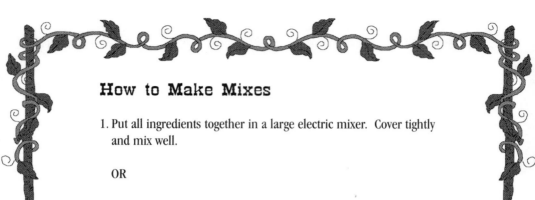

How to Make Mixes

1. Put all ingredients together in a large electric mixer. Cover tightly and mix well.

   OR

2. Shake all ingredients in a large container with a lid or in a plastic bag sealed tightly. If the recipe contains dehydrated whole egg, first combine the egg with one cup of flour in the bag, then add the remaining dry ingredients, close and shake.

How to Store Mixes

1. Store in covered container in dry place. Optimal temperature is 40-68 degrees.

Mini-Mix Recipes

Try a little before making a lot! Experiment with Mini-Mixes to find your family favorites. After making the mix, be sure to measure out the amount of mix called for in the recipe.

Mini-Mixes can be made in a bowl. A wire whisk may be used to blend dry ingredients.

Recipes may need to be adjusted, depending on your altitude or the brand of dehydrated food you use (another reason to try the Mini-Mix before making the full mix).

Important Tips

Mix recipes can be made from either regular or instant powdered milk, using the same proportions. The taste will be the same; however, the nutritional value will differ. To use powdered milk for a drink, you need to use twice as much instant powder as regular powder.

Fructose may be substituted for sugar. For best results, practice using the Mini-Mix, substituting about 1/2 cup fructose to one cup of sugar.

When called for, cream of tartar is a key ingredient in these recipes, so be sure to include it!

Instead of greasing pans, you can also use any commercial pan spray to prevent sticking---a must for waffles!

If dehydrated products (milk, butter, margarine, etc.) become hard or lumpy, break into pieces and process in a blender just long enough to make it a fine powder again.

If you want to ensure a longer shelf life for your mixes, put your flour in the freezer for 2 days before making mixes.

Dehydrated egg white and dehydrated whole egg can be used inter-changeably in most recipes, according to dietary needs and taste.

When making cookie dough or frosting, the batter may seem stiff at first, but it will moisten as you stir. If you add additional water, add only a few drops at a time.

When using dehydrated shortening or whole egg in your favorite family recipes, use the following equivalents: 1 cup prepared shortening = 1/2 cup dehydrated shortening; 1 Tablespoon whole egg plus 3 Tablespoons water = one fresh egg. Add to dry ingredients in mix.

GIFT IDEAS

Looking for a terrific, useful gift? Make a Mix-a-Meal gift for any occasion. The possibilities are endless for Bridal Showers, Weddings, Valentine's Day, Birthdays, Anniversaries, Christmas, and more.

Here are some fun ideas:

Place a Mix-A-Meal Cookbook and ingredients for a recipe in a gift basket, along with utensils, serving spoons, etc.

Put a cookie mix in a decorated cloth bag or decorated box with cookie cutters dangling from ribbon.

Layer ingredients of cookie, cake, or brownie mixes in clear jars. Do not mix together. Top with fabric-decorated lid and add ribbon or raffia. Include directions for using mix.

Here is a fun gift for kids:

PLAY DOUGH MIX
Combine:
6 cups flour
3 cups salt
2 Tbsp. cream of tartar

MINI-MIX
Combine:
1 1/2 cups flour
3/4 cups salt
1 1/2 tsp. cream of tartar

Add desired food coloring to 1 1/2 cups water and 1 1/2 Tbsp. oil. Add 2 1/4 cups Play Dough Mix (above). Bring to a boil, stirring, until mixture forms a thick ball. Knead to desired texture. Store in covered container.

CAMPING IDEAS

Summer camping trips are a snap when you plan ahead with Mix-A-Meal. Make the mixes before the trip and put them in ziplock bags with the directions written on the bag. Here are some fun meal ideas:

Breakfast:
Pancakes (p. 36) with Maple Syrup (p. 38)
Biscuits (p. 13) in Dutch Oven with Country Gravy (p. 47)

Lunch:
Cream of Broccoli Soup (p. 60)
Alfredo Delight (p. 57)
Pocket Bread (p. 28) (make ahead and freeze) with fillings (p. 29)

Dinner:
Barbecue Sauce (p. 44) for any barbecued meat or veggies
Spaghetti Supper (p. 61)

Desserts:
Chocolate Pudding (p. 100) - Refrigerate in ice chest or in cold stream (put rocks around it so the pudding won't float away!)

Yellow Cake (p. 85) in Dutch Oven with melted butter, brown sugar, and pineapple in bottom for Pineapple Upside Down Cake

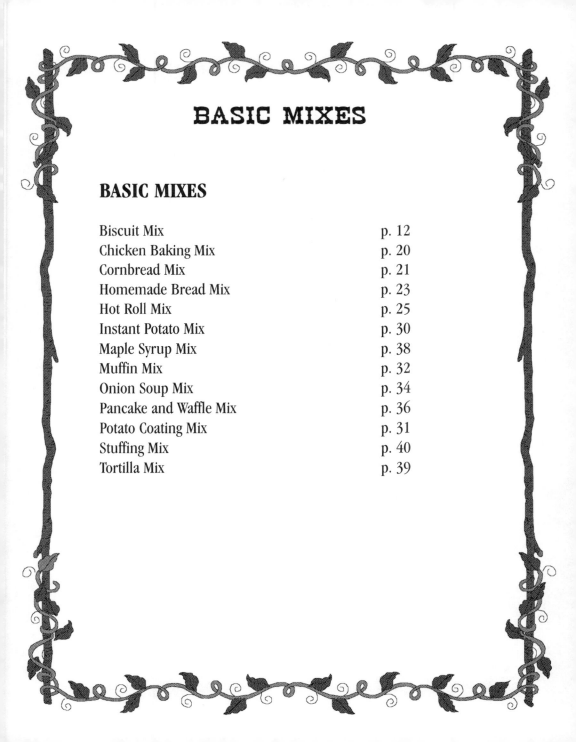

BASIC MIXES

BASIC MIXES

BISCUIT MIX

Combine:

8 1/2 cups flour
1 1/4 cups dehydrated shortening or margarine
3/4 cup powdered milk
1/2 cup dehydrated whole egg
1/4 cup baking powder
1 Tbsp. salt
2 tsp. cream of tartar
1 tsp. baking soda

MINI-MIX

Combine:

2 1/8 cups flour
5 Tbsp. dehydrated shortening or margarine
3 Tbsp. powdered milk
2 Tbsp. dehydrated whole egg
1 scant Tbsp. baking powder
1 tsp. salt
1/2 tsp. cream of tartar
1/4 tsp. baking soda

Drop Biscuits

Combine:

3 cups Biscuit Mix (above)
1 cup water

Stir vigorously until blended and drop by teaspoonsful onto greased baking sheet. Bake at 400 degrees for 10-12 minutes. Makes 12-18 biscuits.

Biscuit Mix can be used in any recipe calling for a commercial biscuit mix. It works well with Dutch Oven recipes also.

Rolled Biscuits

Combine and stir vigorously (20 strokes):
2 cups Biscuit Mix (p. 12)
1/2 cup water

Lightly flour a board with Biscuit Mix and turn all the mixture onto it. Knead to a ball and roll out to 1/2" thickness. Cut with a knife or a cutter dipped in flour. Place 2" apart on a greased baking sheet. Bake at 425 degrees for 10-12 minutes. Makes 12 biscuits.

Pot Pies

Combine:
2 cups diced, cooked turkey, chicken, beef or ham
1-2 cups diced, cooked potatoes or cooked rice
1 cup cooked vegetables: carrots, peas, onions, and celery
2 cups Country Gravy (p. 47) or White Sauce (p. 54)

Spoon hot "stew" combination into a large casserole dish or several individual oven-safe bowls. Roll out Rolled Biscuit Dough (above), place over hot stew and cut steam "vents." Bake at 400 degrees until crust is brown (about 10-12 minutes).

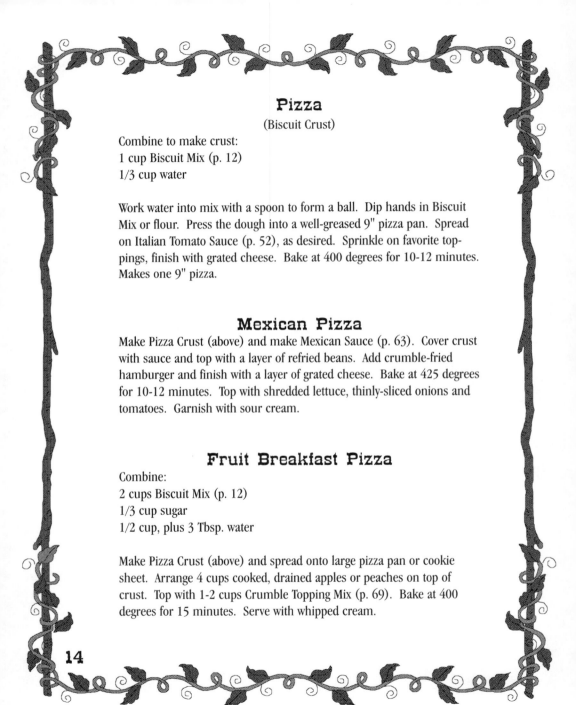

Pizza

(Biscuit Crust)

Combine to make crust:
1 cup Biscuit Mix (p. 12)
1/3 cup water

Work water into mix with a spoon to form a ball. Dip hands in Biscuit
Mix or flour. Press the dough into a well-greased 9" pizza pan. Spread
on Italian Tomato Sauce (p. 52), as desired. Sprinkle on favorite toppings, finish with grated cheese. Bake at 400 degrees for 10-12 minutes.
Makes one 9" pizza.

Mexican Pizza

Make Pizza Crust (above) and make Mexican Sauce (p. 63). Cover crust
with sauce and top with a layer of refried beans. Add crumble-fried
hamburger and finish with a layer of grated cheese. Bake at 425 degrees
for 10-12 minutes. Top with shredded lettuce, thinly-sliced onions and
tomatoes. Garnish with sour cream.

Fruit Breakfast Pizza

Combine:
2 cups Biscuit Mix (p. 12)
1/3 cup sugar
1/2 cup, plus 3 Tbsp. water

Make Pizza Crust (above) and spread onto large pizza pan or cookie
sheet. Arrange 4 cups cooked, drained apples or peaches on top of
crust. Top with 1-2 cups Crumble Topping Mix (p. 69). Bake at 400
degrees for 15 minutes. Serve with whipped cream.

Crackers

Combine:
2 cups Biscuit Mix (p. 12)
1/2 cup cold water

Mix as for Rolled Biscuits, only roll out VERY THIN. Shake a little salt over the rolled dough. Cut with pizza cutter into 4 pieces. Lift with spatula onto greased baking sheet. Cut again with pizza cutter into small pieces about 1/2" square. Bake at 425 degrees for 7-10 minutes.

Caution: Do not over bake crackers; they will crisp as they cool.

VARIATIONS:

CHEESY SNACKS:
2 cups Biscuit Mix (p. 12)
1/4 cup dehydrated cheese
1/2 cup, plus 2 tsp. water

ONION CRACKERS:
2 cups Biscuit Mix (p. 12)
2 tsp. Onion Soup Mix (p. 34)
1/2 cup, plus 2 tsp. water

TACO CRISPS:
2 cups Biscuit Mix (p. 12)
1/2 tsp. taco spices and 1/2 cup water
Shake on seasoned salt (p. 43) before baking

VEGETABLE THINS:
2 cups Biscuit Mix (p. 12)
2 tsp. veggie salt mix (p. 49)
1/2 cup, plus 1 tsp. water

WHOLE WHEAT:
Use Biscuit Mix (p. 12) made with all or part whole wheat flour.
Sprinkle with salt before baking.

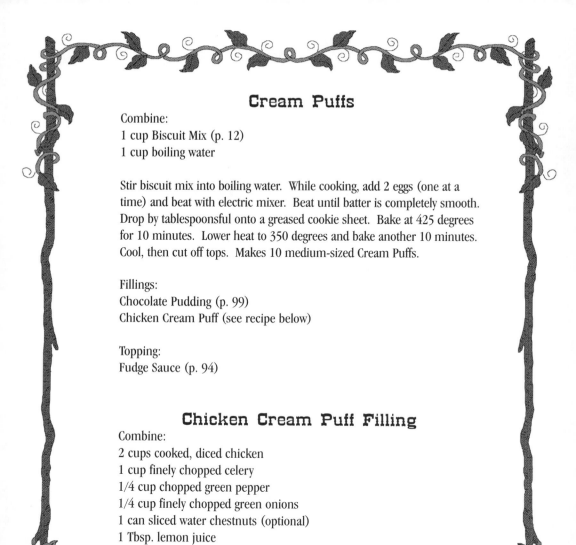

Cream Puffs

Combine:
1 cup Biscuit Mix (p. 12)
1 cup boiling water

Stir biscuit mix into boiling water. While cooking, add 2 eggs (one at a time) and beat with electric mixer. Beat until batter is completely smooth. Drop by tablespoonsful onto a greased cookie sheet. Bake at 425 degrees for 10 minutes. Lower heat to 350 degrees and bake another 10 minutes. Cool, then cut off tops. Makes 10 medium-sized Cream Puffs.

Fillings:
Chocolate Pudding (p. 99)
Chicken Cream Puff (see recipe below)

Topping:
Fudge Sauce (p. 94)

Chicken Cream Puff Filling

Combine:
2 cups cooked, diced chicken
1 cup finely chopped celery
1/4 cup chopped green pepper
1/4 cup finely chopped green onions
1 can sliced water chestnuts (optional)
1 Tbsp. lemon juice
Mayonnaise to desired consistency
Top with sprouts, if desired

Tempura

(this batter makes wonderful, fast onion rings!)

Combine:
3 cups Biscuit Mix (p. 12)
2 scant cups cold water

Slice vegetables thin or meats to bite size and dip into batter:

Zucchini	Onion Slices	Carrots
Parsnips	Green Peppers	Apples
Yams	Mushrooms	Eggplant
Shrimp	Fish	Cheese Cubes

Fry in hot oil, turning once to brown both sides.

Fritters

Combine:
1 cup Biscuit Mix (p. 12)
1/2 cup diced apples, onions, clams or corn
1/4 cup liquid

Drop by teaspoonful into hot oil and fry golden brown on each side.

Braided Dinner Roll

Combine and stir vigorously 20 strokes:
2 cups Biscuit Mix (p. 12)
1/2 cup cold water

Turn mixture onto a board floured with additional Biscuit Mix. Knead lightly and roll dough into an 11" x 14" rectangle pan. Place on lightly-greased cookie sheet. Choose a filling (p. 18) and spoon it down the center of the dough. Cut diagonal strips at 1" intervals from the outside edge to the filling. Fold strips to cross over the top of the filling. Bake at 375 degrees for 15-20 minutes and top with a sauce.

Braided Roll Fillings

Chicken OR Tuna Filling

Combine:
1 can chunk tuna, drained or 1 cup cooked, diced chicken
1/2 cup chopped ripe olives
1/2 cup chopped celery
1/2 cup chopped green pepper
1/2 cup chopped green onions
1/2 cup grated cheese
1/4 cup cream of chicken soup or 1/3 cup White Sauce (p. 54)
After baking, serve with a sauce:
Cheese Sauce (p. 46)
White Sauce (p. 54) or remaining cream of chicken soup

Patty-Melt Filling

Combine:
crumble-fried hamburger
sliced olives
green peppers
sliced onions
swiss cheese
Add:
Tomato sauce (p. 52), Picante' sauce (p. 53), Chili Thick and Fast (p. 62)
After baking, serve with additional sauce.

Pork & Beans Picnic

Drain pork and beans and save sauce for topping.
Add hot dog slices and cheese to beans for filling.

Taco Filling

Combine:
refried beans
crumble-fried hamburger
grated cheese
Picante' sauce (p. 53)
Top with tossed salad and sour cream over each slice.

Breakfast Cake

Combine and mix well:
3 cups Biscuit Mix (p. 12)
1/3 cup sugar
1 1/4 cups water
2 tsp. liquid vanilla

Spread half of the batter into a greased and floured 9" x 9" pan. Add slices of drained, cooked or canned apples or peaches.

Sprinkle 3/4 cup Crumble Topping Mix (p. 69) over the fruit. Add remaining batter and top with 1/4 cup Crumble Topping Mix. Bake at 350 degrees for 40 minutes. Serve hot with whipped cream.

Note: THIS CAKE CAN ALSO BE PREPARED AND REFRIGERATED OVERNIGHT:

Make the cake as directed above. Cover with plastic wrap and place in the refrigerator. The next morning, bake, uncovered, as directed above.

**A FUN SPECIAL
BREAKFAST WITH
NO MORNING FUSS!**

CHICKEN BAKING MIX

Combine:

3 cups flour
2 Tbsp. dehydrated margarine or butter
2 Tbsp. chicken bouillon (soup base)
1 Tbsp. poultry seasoning
1 Tbsp. dehydrated cheese
1 tsp. onion powder
1/4 tsp. garlic powder
1/4 tsp. black pepper

MINI-MIX

Contents:

1 scant cup flour
2 tsp. dehydrated margarine or butter
2 tsp. chicken bouillon (soup base)
1 tsp. dehydrated cheese
1 tsp. poultry seasoning
1/4 tsp. onion powder
pinch of garlic powder
pinch of black pepper

Oven Baked Chicken

Combine:

6-8 pieces chicken
1 cup Chicken Baking Mix in a plastic bag

Dip chicken in water, milk, or whipped egg (for a thicker coating). Shake chicken pieces in a plastic bag, one at a time, to coat with mix. Bake at 350 degrees on foil-lined cookie sheet for 1 hour or until golden brown.

CORNBREAD MIX

Combine:

5 cups whole wheat or white flour
5 cups cornmeal
3 1/3 cups white or brown sugar
1 1/3 cups dehydrated margarine or butter
1/4 cup powdered milk or powdered buttermilk
1/2 cup dehydrated egg white or whole egg*
2 1/2 tsp. baking soda
2 1/2 tsp. baking powder
2 1/2 tsp. salt

MINI-MIX

Combine:

1 1/4 cup whole wheat or white flour
1 1/4 cup cornmeal
3/4 cup white or brown sugar
1/3 rounded cup dehydrated margarine or shortening
2 Tbsp. powdered milk or powdered buttermilk
1 1/2 Tbsp. dehydrated egg white or whole egg*
1/2 rounded tsp. baking soda
1/2 rounded tsp. baking powder
1/2 tsp. salt

*Using dehydrated egg white instead of dehydrated whole egg gives the corn-bread a lighter taste, but either works well. You can also leave the dehydrated egg out of the mix and whip 1 fresh egg as part of the liquid measurement.

NOTE: You can grind whole dried corn in your wheat grinder to make your own finely-textured cornmeal. It is recommended that you grind at least 1 cup of wheat afterwards to clean the grinder stones.

Cornbread

Combine:
3 cups Cornbread Mix (p. 21)
1 cup water

Bake at 350 degrees in an 8" x 8" greased pan for 30-40 minutes or bake in greased muffin tins for 20 minutes at 350 degrees. Serve with honey butter.

Honey Butter

Stir together:
1 cup honey
1/2 cup dehydrated butter

High-Rise Cornbread

Combine:
3 cups Cornbread Mix (p. 21)
2 cups fresh buttermilk

Bake in an 8" x 8" greased pan at 350 degrees for 30-40 minutes.

Cornbread Plus

Combine:
2 Tbsp. dehydrated egg white
1/4 cup water

Whip for 1 minute until peaks form. Lumps will dissolve as egg whites are whipped.

Add:
3 cups Cornbread Mix (p. 21)
1 cup water

Fold into whipped egg whites. Bake in an 8" x 8" greased pan at 350 degrees for 30-40 minutes.

HOMEMADE BREAD MIX

Combine:
8 cups sugar
4 cups dehydrated shortening
1 cup salt

Note: This mix makes over 60 loaves of either white or whole wheat bread!

MINI-MIX

Combine:
1/2 cup sugar
1/4 cup dehydrated shortening
1 Tbsp. salt

Homemade Bread

Sprinkle 2 Tablespoons yeast into 2 cups warm water. Let stand until yeast dissolves and begins to foam.

Add:
3 cups warm water
3/4 cups Homemade Bread Mix (above)
3/4 cups vital wheat gluten, optional

Knead in about 10-11 cups of flour to make a soft dough. Continue kneading for 8-10 minutes. Shape and place in four well-greased medium-sized bread pans. Let rise until double in bulk, about 25-45 minutes. Bake at 350 degrees for 30-35 minutes. Remove loaves from pans and place side by side on a towel. Cover completely with the towel and place on a rack to cool. Makes 4 medium loaves.

Scones: Pinch off desired amount of dough and roll to 1/4" thickness. Cut into desired shapes and fry in hot grease until browned.

Note: Store yeast in the freezer for longer life.

Bread Maker Whole Wheat Bread

If you have a single loaf Bread Maker, you will love this mix!

Combine ingredients in your bread maker pan in this order:
1 1/4 cups water
1/4 cup Homemade Bread Mix (p. 23)
3 cups white bread flour
2 tsp. active dry yeast

Bake according to bread maker's instructions.

For whole wheat bread, follow above instructions combining:
2 1/2 cups whole wheat flour (Golden 86 wheat flour works great!)
1/2 cup vital wheat gluten
2 tsp. active dry yeast

Why Use Gluten?

Gluten is the ingredient that gives bread a finer texture and allows it to rise higher, especially in a bread maker. It is one of the key ingredients in costly individual bread mixes.

HOT ROLL MIX

Combine:
10 cups flour
1 cup dehydrated margarine or butter
2/3 cups sugar
1/4 cup powdered milk
2 Tbsp. salt

MINI-MIX

Combine:
3 1/3 cups flour
1/3 cup dehydrated margarine or butter
1/4 cup sugar
1 heaping Tbsp. powdered milk
2 tsp. salt

Note: A 30-pound plastic storage bucket holds four Hot Roll Mixes. Just prepare a regular mix and pour it into the bucket. Repeat this process three more times and the bucket will be full, a MAXI-MIX!

Basic Roll Dough

Combine:
1 1/2 cups warm water
1 Tbsp. active dry yeast

Add a sprinkle of sugar to activate yeast (optional). Let rise for 3-5 minutes.

Add:
4 cups Hot Roll Mix (above)

Knead 5-10 minutes until smooth and satiny. Let rise in a bowl for one hour (this step is optional). Roll out and shape rolls on a greased baking sheet
OR
Pinch off in 3" rounds and place side-by-side in a greased 9" x 13" pan. Let rise for one hour or until double in size. Bake at 375 degrees for 15 minutes. Lightly cover with foil the last 5 minutes.

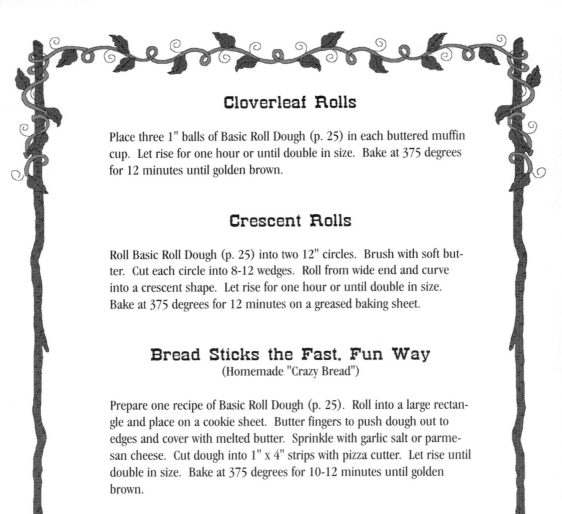

Cloverleaf Rolls

Place three 1" balls of Basic Roll Dough (p. 25) in each buttered muffin cup. Let rise for one hour or until double in size. Bake at 375 degrees for 12 minutes until golden brown.

Crescent Rolls

Roll Basic Roll Dough (p. 25) into two 12" circles. Brush with soft butter. Cut each circle into 8-12 wedges. Roll from wide end and curve into a crescent shape. Let rise for one hour or until double in size. Bake at 375 degrees for 12 minutes on a greased baking sheet.

Bread Sticks the Fast, Fun Way
(Homemade "Crazy Bread")

Prepare one recipe of Basic Roll Dough (p. 25). Roll into a large rectangle and place on a cookie sheet. Butter fingers to push dough out to edges and cover with melted butter. Sprinkle with garlic salt or parmesan cheese. Cut dough into 1" x 4" strips with pizza cutter. Let rise until double in size. Bake at 375 degrees for 10-12 minutes until golden brown.

These taste wonderful dipped in spaghetti sauce or Italian Tomato Sauce (p. 52).

Cinnamon Rolls

Roll Basic Roll Dough (p. 25) into a 6" x 20" rectangle. Brush with soft butter. Sprinkle generously with Crumble Topping Mix (p. 106) and raisins. Roll up and cut* into about 18 slices. Place cut side down in greased baking pan or in buttered muffin cups. Bake at 375 degrees for 12 minutes. Glaze with Butter Cream Frosting (p. 90) while hot.

*Tip: Slide dental floss under dough, cross the ends and pull for a very clean cut.

Bundt Sweet Roll Bread
(A beautiful gift!)

Prepare one basic recipe of Cinnamon Rolls (see above). Instead of cutting, place the roll in a buttered Bundt pan, seam side up. Seal the two ends together, making it as even as possible. Let rise until double in size. Bake at 375 degrees for 20-25 minutes. Invert bread onto a serving platter. Glaze while hot with Butter Cream Frosting (p. 90) and sprinkle with sliced almonds.

Heavenly Orange Rolls

Prepare one basic recipe of Basic Roll Dough (p. 25). Roll into 6" x 20" rectangle and spread with melted butter. Sprinkle with 1/3 to 1/2 cup sugar. Add grated peel from 1 large orange or 1/3 cup orange granules.

Place in muffin tins with one teaspoon of melted butter in each muffin cup. Let rise until double in size. Bake at 375 degrees for 10-12 minutes. Glaze while hot with Lemon Butter Cream Glaze (p. 91).

Pizza
(Party Size!)

Spread half of the Basic Roll Dough (p. 25) on a greased cookie sheet. Cover with Italian Tomato Sauce (p. 52). Add your favorite toppings and grated mozzarella cheese. Bake at 375 degrees for 12-15 minutes until cheese bubbles and edges brown.

Tips: Grease pan or sprinkle cornmeal on the pan for easy crust removal. Grease your hands to press the dough out evenly in the pan.

Pocket Bread

Combine:
3/4 cup warm water
1/2 Tbsp. yeast

Yeast will activate faster with a little sugar sprinkled on top. Combine and let stand for 3-5 minutes. Add 2 cups Hot Roll Mix (p. 25). Knead 5-10 minutes. Cover and let rise for one hour. Divide dough into six 3" balls and place on a greased baking sheet. Roll with the side of a glass or press out with fingers to 4" circles. Bake immediately in 400-degree oven for 5 to 7 minutes. Let cool 10 minutes before cutting tops (kitchen scissors work great!). Stuff with your choice of Pocket Bread Fillings (p. 29).

POCKET BREAD FILLINGS

Basic Salad Filling

Combine any of the following (finely sliced):
Lettuce, cucumbers, avocado, tomatoes, celery, green onions, green peppers, mushrooms, alfalfa sprouts.

Mix vegetables together with mayonnaise and lemon juice
OR
Layer vegetables in the pocket bread and top with favorite dressing.
Garnish with grated cheese.

Deluxe Pocket Bread Fillings

Add to Basic Salad Filling (above) cooked, diced chicken, ham, bacon, chipped beef or hard-boiled eggs. Garnish with chicken or bacon textured vegetable protein (TVP), optional.

Taco Filling

Layer in the pocket bread:
crumble-fried hamburger
grated cheese
shredded lettuce
Picanté Sauce (p. 53)
Bean Dip (p. 53)

Top with sour cream.

INSTANT POTATO MIX
Combine:
6 scant cups dehydrated margarine
3 cups powdered milk
1/2 scant cup salt
1/3 cup dehydrated cheese
1 Tbsp. onion powder

MINI-MIX
Combine:
3 Tbsp. dehydrated margarine
1 1/2 Tbsp. powdered milk
3/4 tsp. salt
1/2 tsp. dehydrated cheese
1/8 tsp. onion powder

Instant Potatoes
(Use this mix instead of adding fresh milk and butter to instant potatoes)

Combine with wire whisk:
1 1/2 cups hottest tap water (adjust water, if needed, for the brand of
potatoes used)
1/4 cup Instant Potato Mix (above)

Add:
1 cup instant potato flakes. Cover and let sit for a minute. Stir gently
and serve.

Option: For a wonderful flavor, fold in 2 Tbsp. Dip for Chips or Veggies
(p. 34).

Fresh Mashed Potatoes

When whipping fresh cooked potatoes, add Instant Potato Mix (above)
and water to desired flavor and consistency. Potatoes will have a creamy,
rich texture.

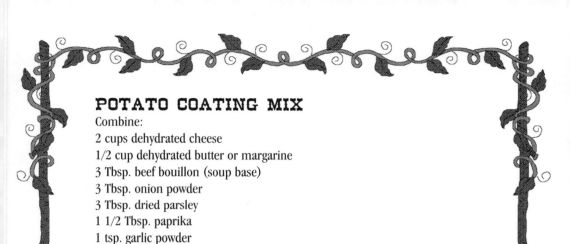

POTATO COATING MIX

Combine:

2 cups dehydrated cheese

1/2 cup dehydrated butter or margarine

3 Tbsp. beef bouillon (soup base)

3 Tbsp. onion powder

3 Tbsp. dried parsley

1 1/2 Tbsp. paprika

1 tsp. garlic powder

1 tsp. pepper

MINI-MIX

Combine:

2 Tbsp. dehydrated cheese

1/2 Tbsp. dehydrated butter or margarine

1 tsp. beef bouillon (soup base)

1 tsp. onion powder

1 tsp. dried parsley

1/2 tsp. paprika

1/8 tsp. garlic powder

1/8 tsp. pepper

Oven-Fried Potatoes

Peel and dice 6 medium potatoes. Pour 2 Tbsp. cooking oil (or water) into a plastic bag. Add potatoes and coat pieces. Process 2 slices of toast in a blender to make fine bread crumbs. Add bread crumbs and 1/4 cup Potato Coating Mix (above) to bag and shake. Place potatoes on a sprayed cookie sheet. Bake at 375 degrees for 30 minutes.

Variation: Add 1 Tbsp. taco seasoning.

MUFFIN MIX

Combine:

8 cups white or whole wheat flour
2 1/2 cups brown or white sugar
1 1/4 cups dehydrated shortening
1/2 cup powdered milk
1/3 cup baking powder
1 1/2 tsp. salt

MINI-MIX

Combine:

2 1/4 cups white or whole wheat flour
1/3 cup brown or white sugar
1/4 cup dehydrated shortening
3 Tbsp. powdered milk
1 1/2 Tbsp. baking powder
1/2 scant tsp. salt

Muffins

Blend one fresh egg and enough water to make 2 cups liquid. Add 3 1/8 cups Muffin Mix (above). Blend well with a wire whisk, but do not beat. Fill 9-10 buttered muffin cups almost full. Bake 20 minutes at 425 degrees.
OR
Spread in an 8" x 8" greased pan. Bake at 400 degrees for 25-35 minutes.

Optional: Before baking, add 1/2 cup raisins or blueberries or top with brown sugar and chopped nuts.

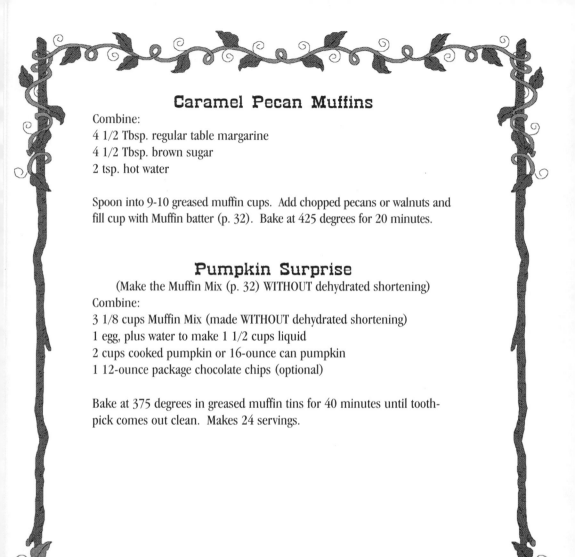

Caramel Pecan Muffins

Combine:

4 1/2 Tbsp. regular table margarine
4 1/2 Tbsp. brown sugar
2 tsp. hot water

Spoon into 9-10 greased muffin cups. Add chopped pecans or walnuts and fill cup with Muffin batter (p. 32). Bake at 425 degrees for 20 minutes.

Pumpkin Surprise

(Make the Muffin Mix (p. 32) WITHOUT dehydrated shortening)

Combine:

3 1/8 cups Muffin Mix (made WITHOUT dehydrated shortening)
1 egg, plus water to make 1 1/2 cups liquid
2 cups cooked pumpkin or 16-ounce can pumpkin
1 12-ounce package chocolate chips (optional)

Bake at 375 degrees in greased muffin tins for 40 minutes until toothpick comes out clean. Makes 24 servings.

ONION SOUP MIX

Combine:

2/3 cup dehydrated chopped onions
1/2 cup beef bouillon (soup base)
1/2 cup dehydrated butter or margarine
2 Tbsp. cornstarch
2 tsp. onion powder
2 tsp. parsley flakes (optional)

Mix well and store in quart jar. Use in any dry onion soup recipe.

Dip for Chips or Veggies

Combine:

2 tsp. Onion Soup Mix (above)
1 cup (8 oz.) sour cream (fat free works great!)

Onion Steamed Rice

Combine:

1 cup rice to 3 cups water
2 tsp. Onion Soup Mix (above)

Cover and steam 20 minutes until rice is tender and dry.

Pasta Perfect

Combine:

1 Tbsp. butter
2 tsp. Onion Soup Mix (above)

Saute' one minute and add 2 cups cooked fettuccine or egg noodles. Stir until warmed through and serve.

Roast Beef Supreme

Sprinkle 1-2 tsp. Onion Soup Mix (p. 34) into crock pot. Place a 3-4 pound beef roast on top of the mix. Sprinkle 1-2 tsp. Onion Soup Mix over the top of the roast. Add 2 cups water and cover. Cook for 8-12 hours on medium heat.

OR

Cook for 3 hours on high, and then 6-8 more hours on low.

French Onion Soup

Combine:

1 cup water

1/2 cup Caramelized Onions (see recipe below)

2 tsp. Onion Soup Mix (p. 34)

Caramelized Onions

Cook fresh, chopped onions or thinly-sliced onions with a little water in a pan and let them boil dry. Watch carefully, and as soon as they begin to brown, add a little more water. As you stir the onions in the water, they will absorb the brown from the bottom of the pan, giving them a sweet, beefy flavor. You can repeat this procedure as many times as you wish for desired tenderness. These onions add a wonderful flavor to any homemade soup or stew.

PANCAKE AND WAFFLE MIX

Combine:

8 cups white or whole wheat flour
3/4 cup dehydrated shortening
3/4 cup powdered milk
3/4 cup brown or white sugar or 1/3 cup fructose
2/3 cup dehydrated whole eggs
1/3 cup baking powder
1 scant Tbsp. salt

MINI-MIX

Combine:

1 cup white or whole wheat flour
1 1/2 Tbsp. dehydrated shortening
1 1/2 Tbsp. powdered milk
1 1/2 Tbsp. brown or white sugar or 1/2 Tbsp. fructose
1 Tbsp. dehydrated whole egg
1 tsp. baking powder
1/8 tsp. salt

Pancakes or Waffles
(Light & Fluffy!)

Combine:

1 scant cup Pancake Mix (above)
1 cup water

Let stand a minute and cook on a hot, oiled griddle. Try spooning pancakes with a gravy ladle for uniform size. Turn when bubbles break on top. Makes six 4" pancakes. Serve with homemade Maple Syrup (p. 38).

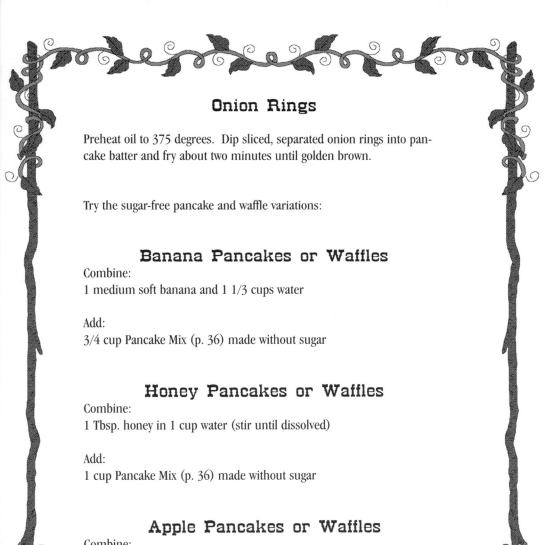

Onion Rings

Preheat oil to 375 degrees. Dip sliced, separated onion rings into pancake batter and fry about two minutes until golden brown.

Try the sugar-free pancake and waffle variations:

Banana Pancakes or Waffles

Combine:
1 medium soft banana and 1 1/3 cups water

Add:
3/4 cup Pancake Mix (p. 36) made without sugar

Honey Pancakes or Waffles

Combine:
1 Tbsp. honey in 1 cup water (stir until dissolved)

Add:
1 cup Pancake Mix (p. 36) made without sugar

Apple Pancakes or Waffles

Combine:
1 cup Pancake Mix (p. 36) made without sugar

Add:
1 cup apple juice

MAPLE SYRUP MIX

Combine:

6 cups white sugar

2 cups brown sugar

1 tsp. powdered maple syrup flavoring

1/2 tsp. powdered vanilla flavoring

MINI-MIX

Combine:

1 1/2 cups white sugar

1/2 cup brown sugar

1/4 tsp. powdered maple syrup flavoring

1/8 tsp. powdered vanilla flavoring

Maple Syrup

Combine:

2 cups Maple Syrup Mix

1 cup water

Stir until mixture boils. Cover and simmer gently for 10 minutes. Syrup will thicken when refrigerated.

Maple Syrup
(without a mix)

Combine:

3 1/2 cups sugar

1/2 cup brown sugar

2 cups water

Stir until mixture boils. Cover and simmer for 10 minutes.

Add:

1 tsp. liquid maple flavoring

1/2 tsp. liquid vanilla flavoring

TORTILLA MIX

Combine:
8 cups flour
2 cups dehydrated shortening
3 Tbsp. powdered milk
1 1/2 Tbsp. salt

MINI-MIX

Combine:
1 cup flour
1/4 cup dehydrated shortening
1 tsp. powdered milk
1/2 tsp. salt

Tortillas

Combine:
1 cup Tortilla Mix (above)
1/3 cup water

Stir vigorously. Turn out on floured board and knead into a ball. Divide in thirds and roll into 6" rounds. Heat in ungreased hot pan, turning until light brown spots appear. Use for the Mexican Dinner recipe (p. 63), or for soft-shelled tacos. These are also delicious when fried until crisp in hot oil, turning once. Sprinkle with cinnamon sugar and serve for dessert.

Baked Enchiladas

Fill Tortillas with Chili, Thick and Fast (p. 62), or cooked beef or chicken. Add Picante' Sauce (p. 53) (optional) and roll up, folding the ends. Combine 2 cups prepared Tomato Sauce (p. 52) with 1 tsp. chili powder. Spread 1 cup of sauce over the bottom of a 9" x 13" baking pan. Add filled tortillas and cover with the remaining cup of Tomato Sauce. Bake at 350 degrees for 30 minutes and cover with grated cheese. Serve with lettuce, sour cream and/or guacamole.

STUFFING MIX

Combine:
1/2 cup Onion Soup Mix (p. 34)
1/2 cup dried parsley flakes
1/4 cup sage
1 Tbsp. chicken bouillon (soup base)
1/2 Tbsp. thyme (optional)

MINI-MIX

Combine:
1 Tbsp. Onion Soup Mix (p. 34)
1 Tbsp. parsley flakes
1/2 tsp. sage
1/2 tsp. chicken bouillon (soup base)
1/4 tsp. thyme (optional)

Quick and Easy Stuffing

Combine in bowl or plastic bag:
2 cups dried bread cubes (p. 41)
2 1/2 Tbsp. Stuffing Mix (above)

Shake or stir to mix evenly. Add 1/3 to 2/3 cup hot water and let sit for 5 minutes. Add 1/4 cup each: chopped celery, onions, water chestnuts (optional). If you desire tender veggies instead of crisp, microwave them first with a little water in a covered dish and then add to stuffing. Bake in covered casserole dish at 350 degrees for 15 minutes.
OR
Microwave on medium 5-10 minutes in a covered pan or dish.

Note: It is not recommended that stuffing be baked inside the turkey.

BREAD CUBES

Cut into cubes:
Day-old toast, muffins, bread, buns, etc. Dry thoroughly and store in covered container until ready to use.

Stuffed Patties Supreme
(A great way to use left-over stuffing!)

Combine:
2 lbs. lean ground hamburger or turkey burger
2 eggs and 1/2 cup milk or water
1 cup bread crumbs
2 tsp. salt
1/4 tsp. pepper

Make 16 patties, pressing mixture between 2 plates with wax paper. Place 8 patties side-by-side in large baking pan. Top each with 1/4 cup prepared stuffing (p. 40). Add 1 slice Swiss or processed cheese (optional). Cover with remaining meat patties and seal the edges. Bake patties uncovered at 400 degrees for 25 minutes.

Gravy

Combine and pour over browned meat patties:
2 1/2 cups water
1 cup White Sauce Mix (p. 54)
1 Tbsp. Onion Soup Mix (p. 34)

Cover and bake at 350 degrees with gravy for another 25 minutes until done. Remove patties and stir the gravy. Make sure you work in all of the drippings from the bottom of the pan. Serve with cooked potatoes or Onion Steamed Rice (p. 34).

Chicken with Gravy

Bake chicken pieces at 375 degrees for 45 minutes in sprayed baking pan. Make gravy (see above) and bake for another 20 minutes.

BASIC MIXES

SAUCES AND SPICE MIXES

BAKING SPICE MIX

Combine:
8 Tbsp. cinnamon
2 Tbsp. nutmeg
1 Tbsp. allspice
1 tsp. cloves (optional)

MINI-MIX

Combine:
1 tsp. cinnamon
1/4 tsp. nutmeg
1/8 tsp. allspice
pinch of cloves (optional)

SEASONED SALT MIX

Combine:
2 cups salt
3/4 cup sugar
1/4 cup dehydrated cheese
1/4 cup taco seasoning
3 Tbsp. onion powder
1 Tbsp. garlic powder
1 Tbsp. thyme
1 Tbsp. paprika

MINI-MIX

Combine:
1/2 cup salt
3 Tbsp. sugar
1 Tbsp. dehydrated cheese
1 Tbsp. taco seasoning
2 tsp. onion powder
1 tsp. garlic powder
1 tsp. thyme
1 tsp. paprika

BARBECUE SAUCE MIX

Combine:
1 1/4 cups sugar
1 1/4 cups tomato powder
1/3 cup onion powder
1 1/2 tsp. dry mustard
1 1/4 tsp. garlic powder
1/2 tsp. cloves
1/8 tsp. cinnamon

MINI-MIX

Combine:
2 Tbsp. sugar
2 Tbsp. tomato powder
1 1/2 rounded tsp. onion powder
1/4 tsp. dry mustard
1/8 tsp. garlic powder
1/16 tsp. cloves
pinch of cinnamon

Barbecue Sauce

Combine:
1/4 cup Barbecue Sauce Mix (above)
1/4 cup Tomato Sauce Mix (p. 52)

Add to:
1 cup BOILING water
1/2 Tbsp. cider vinegar

Stir until thick.

Note: This recipe is mild enough to substitute for ketchup.

44

CATALINA DRESSING MIX

Combine:

4 cups sugar
2 Tbsp. dry mustard
2 Tbsp. salt
2 Tbsp. onion powder
2 Tbsp. celery salt
1 Tbsp. parsley
1 Tbsp. black pepper
1 Tbsp. garlic powder

MINI-MIX

Combine:

2/3 cup sugar
1 tsp. dry mustard
1 tsp. salt
1 tsp. onion powder
1 tsp. celery salt
1/2 tsp. parsley
1/2 tsp. black pepper
1/2 tsp. garlic powder

Catalina Dressing

Combine in blender:

3/4 cup vinegar
3/4 cup Catalina Dressing Mix (above)
1 tsp. molasses

While blender is running, gradually add 1 1/2 cups cooking or salad oil.
Combine in small pan and mix vigorously:

1 1/2 cups BOILING water
1/2 cup tomato powder

Add tomato mixture to ingredients and blend. Add 1 tsp. parsley
(optional). Store in refrigerator.

CHEESE SAUCE MIX

Combine:

4 1/2 cups dehydrated cheese

2 2/3 cups powdered milk

2 2/3 cups dehydrated butter or margarine

2 2/3 cups flour

2 tsp. onion powder

MINI-MIX

Combine:

1/3 cup dehydrated cheese powder

3 Tbsp. powdered milk

3 Tbsp. dehydrated butter or margarine

3 Tbsp. flour

1/8 tsp. onion powder

Cheese Sauce

Combine:

1 cup hot tap water

1/2 cup Cheese Sauce Mix (above)

Bring to a boil, stirring with a wire whisk (it only takes a minute!). For a touch of color, add a few parsley flakes (optional). Use this sauce for: Nacho chips, macaroni and cheese, cheese and broccoli, toppings for a potato bar, or any favorite cheese sauce recipe.

COUNTRY GRAVY MIX

Combine:

6 cups flour

4 cups powdered milk

1 1/2 cups dehydrated butter or margarine

3/4 cup beef bouillon (soup base)

1/2 cup dehydrated chopped onions (optional)

2 Tbsp. onion powder

1 1/2 tsp. ground sage

1 1/2 tsp. ground thyme

MINI-MIX

Combine:

1/2 cup flour

1/3 cup powdered milk

2 Tbsp. dehydrated butter or margarine

1 Tbsp. beef bouillon (soup base)

1/2 Tbsp. dehydrated chopped onions (optional)

1/2 tsp. onion powder

1/8 tsp. ground sage

1/8 tsp. ground thyme

Country Gravy

Combine and whisk smooth in saucepan:

3 cups hot water

1 cup Country Gravy Mix (above)

Bring to a boil, stirring constantly, until thickened (It cooks up fast!)
Add more water, if necessary, for desired consistency. This is great over
chicken-fried steaks or combined with crumble-fried hamburger,
chunks of leftover turkey or chicken. Serve on biscuits, potatoes or rice.

47

FRENCH DRESSING MIX

Combine:
1 1/2 cups sugar
1/2 cup dehydrated cheese
1-2 Tbsp. dry mustard
1 Tbsp. salt
1 Tbsp. paprika
1 Tbsp. onion powder
1 Tbsp. celery salt
1/2 to 1 tsp. black pepper
1/2 to 1 tsp. garlic powder

MINI-MIX

Combine:
1/2 cup sugar
3 Tbsp. dehydrated cheese
1-2 tsp. dry mustard
1 tsp. salt
1 tsp. paprika
1 tsp. onion powder
1 tsp. celery salt
1/4 tsp. black pepper
1/4 tsp. garlic powder

French Creamy Dressing

Mix in a blender:
3/4 cup vinegar
1/4 cup water
3/4 cup French Dressing Mix (above)
1 tsp. molasses (optional)

While blender is running, GRADUALLY add 1 1/2 cups cooking or salad oil.

Combine in a small pan and mix vigorously:
3/4 cup BOILING water
1/4 cup Tomato Sauce Mix (p. 52)
OR
Use one cup tomato paste or ketchup

Add tomato mixture to blender and mix just until blended. Store in the refrigerator.

Note: To reduce fat, may substitute 1 1/2 cups canned applesauce or reconstituted dehydrated applesauce for the oil.

ITALIAN SPICE MIX

Combine:

1/4 cup crushed basil leaf

1/4 cup ground oregano

2 Tbsp. garlic powder

1/2 cup parsley

MINI-MIX

Combine:

1/8 tsp. crushed basil leaf

1/8 tsp. ground oregano

1/16 tsp. garlic powder

1/4 tsp. parsley

This can be used in any recipe calling for Italian Seasoning.

VEGGIE SALT MIX

Combine:

1/2 cup vegetable powder*

1/4 cup salt

1 1/2 Tbsp. dill weed (optional)

MINI-MIX

Combine:

2 Tbsp. vegetable powder*

1 Tbsp. salt

1 tsp. dill weed (optional)

Combine powder, salt and dill and use in a salt shaker.

*Vegetable powder: Put 1/2 cup dehydrated vegetable stew in a blender and process until fine. Pour into a strainer and shake to separate vegetable powder from the large pieces remaining.

49

RANCH DRESSING MIX

Combine:

1 cup powdered milk or powdered buttermilk
6 Tbsp. onion powder
3 Tbsp garlic powder
3 Tbsp. parsley (crushed)
1 1/2 Tbsp. beef bouillon (soup base)
1 1/2 Tbsp. chicken bouillon (soup base)
1 1/2 Tbsp. black pepper
1 1/2 Tbsp. celery seed
1 1/2 Tbsp. dehydrated cheese

MINI-MIX

Combine:

2 1/2 Tbsp. powdered milk or powdered buttermilk
1 Tbsp. onion powder
1 1/2 tsp. garlic powder
1 1/2 tsp. crushed parsley
1 tsp. beef bouillon (soup base)
1 tsp. chicken bouillon (soup base)
1 tsp. black pepper
1 tsp. celery seed
1 tsp. dehydrated cheese

Ranch Dressing

Combine:

1 cup fat-free sour cream
1-2 Tbsp. skim milk
1-2 Tbsp. vinegar
3 Tbsp. Ranch Dressing Mix (above)

Ranch Dressing Deluxe

Combine:

1 cup salad dressing, mayonnaise, or sour cream
1/4 cup fresh buttermilk
1/2 cup cottage cheese
1/3 cup Ranch Dressing Mix (above)
1-2 Tbsp. vinegar

Tastes great on baked potatoes! Flavor improves with refrigeration.

SALAD DRESSING MIX
Combine:
3 cups sugar
1 1/2 cups powdered milk or buttermilk
1 1/2 cups powdered cheese
1/4 cup onion powder
2 Tbsp. dry mustard
2 Tbsp. salt
2 Tbsp. garlic powder
2 Tbsp. celery salt
1 Tbsp. pepper

MINI-MIX
Combine:
1/2 cup sugar
1/4 cup each powdered milk or buttermilk
1/4 cup powdered cheese
2 tsp. onion powder
1 tsp. dry mustard
1 tsp. salt
1 tsp. garlic powder
1 tsp. celery salt
1/2 tsp. pepper

Salad Dressing
Combine in a blender:
1/2 cup Salad Dressing Mix (above)
1/2 cup water and 1/3 cup vinegar

While blender is running, GRADUALLY add 3/4 cup oil.

House Dressing
Make Salad Dressing (above). Thin as desired, and add poppy seeds.

Thousand Island Dressing
Make Salad Dressing (above)
Add:
1/2 cup prepared Barbecue Sauce (p. 44)
1 grated boiled egg, and approximately 1 Tablespoon chopped sweet
pickles. Thin with sweet pickle juice to desired consistency.

TOMATO SAUCE MIX

Combine:

6 3/4 cups tomato powder
1 1/2 cups dehydrated cheese
1 1/8 cups sugar
3/4 cup beef bouillon (soup base)
3/4 cup cornstarch

MINI-MIX

Combine:

3 Tbsp. tomato powder
2 tsp. dehydrated cheese
1 1/2 tsp. sugar
1 tsp. beef bouillon (soup base)
1 tsp. cornstarch

Tomato Sauce

1 scant cup BOILING water
1/4 cup Tomato Sauce Mix (above)

Important: Add Tomato Sauce Mix all at once to the boiling water. The water must be boiling or the sauce will not thicken. Remove from heat and stir vigorously with a wire whisk. Makes approximately 1 cup.

Italian Tomato Sauce

Add 1/2 tsp. Italian Spice Mix (p. 49) to 1 cup boiling water. Add 1/4 cup Tomato Sauce Mix (above) and stir vigorously. Use for Pizza and as a dip for breadsticks.

Picante' Sauce

Combine and bring to boil for one minute:
2 cups water
1/2 cup chopped green pepper
1/4 cup chopped onion

Stir 1/2 cup Tomato Sauce Mix (p. 52) into boiling mixture.

Remove from heat and add:
1 small can chopped green chilies and juice
1 cup drained stewed or fresh chopped tomatoes
Add a little Tabasco if you like it hot.

Picante' Nacho Sauce

Combine:
1 cup hot water
1/2 cup Cheese Sauce Mix (p. 46)

Cook until thick and add 1 cup Picante' Sauce (above). While hot, add
1/2-1 cup sour cream (optional). Serve over chips with lettuce topping.

Bean Dip

Cook any dried beans (pinto or chili beans are preferred). Mash them
as you would for refried beans. Add Picante' Sauce or Picante' Nacho
Sauce to desired consistency.

WHITE SAUCE MIX

Combine:
4 cups powdered milk
4 cups flour
4 cups dehydrated margarine or butter
2 tsp. salt

MINI-MIX

1/4 cup powdered milk
1/4 cup flour
1/4 cup dehydrated margarine or butter
1/8 tsp. salt

Basic White Sauce

Combine in a sauce pan:
1/2 cup White Sauce Mix (above)
1 cup hot tap water
salt and pepper as desired

Bring to boil in sauce pan. With wire whisk stir constantly over medium heat until thick to prevent scorching.

Use White Sauce Mix for:
Creamed soups and chowders, scalloped potatoes, white gravy, Creamed Vegetables (p. 55) and chicken a la king. To extend canned creamed soups as a delicious casserole base, use 2 parts Basic White Sauce to 1 part cream of chicken, mushroom, or celery soup.

Creamed Vegetables

Soak 1/2 cup dehydrated vegetables for 20 minutes in 2 cups water. Add
1 Tbsp. Onion Soup Mix (p. 34). Simmer for 20 minutes or until vegetables are tender
OR
Steam 1 cup fresh vegetables to desired consistency. Any canned vegetables also work well. Drain water from cooked vegetables. Add enough
hot water to make 1 1/2 cups liquid. Stir in 3/4 cup White Sauce Mix (p.
54). Cook until thick, stirring constantly. Combine cooked vegetables
and sauce, stirring gently. Serve over baked or mashed potatoes, rice or
toast. Garnish with sliced boiled egg, bacon bits or crumble fried bacon,
if desired.

Creamy Casseroles

Prepare creamed vegetables from above recipe using these proportions:
3 cups total liquid and 1 1/2 cups White Sauce Mix (p. 54)
Add:
2 cups cooked chicken, turkey pieces or diced ham
1 cup Onion Steamed Rice (p. 34) or cooked noodles
Cover with grated cheese and bake until cheese has melted.

Cheesy Creamed Vegetables

Substitute Cheese Sauce Mix (p. 46) in place of the White Sauce Mix.

BASIC MIXES

INSTANT MEALS

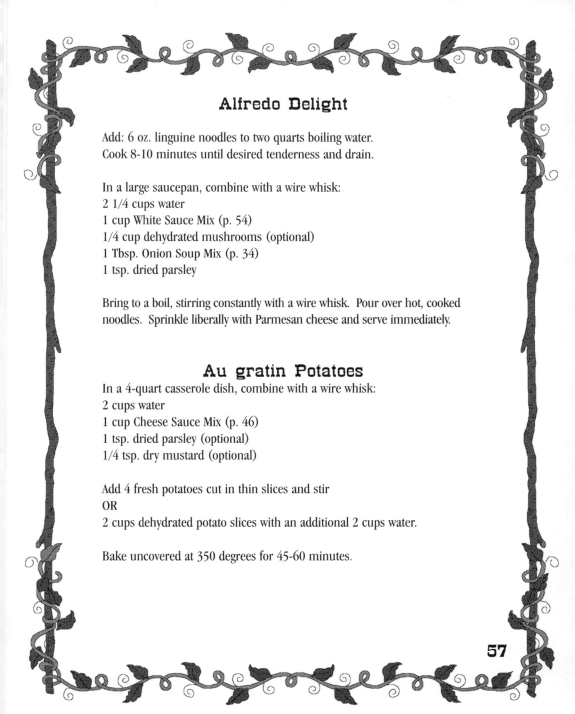

Alfredo Delight

Add: 6 oz. linguine noodles to two quarts boiling water.
Cook 8-10 minutes until desired tenderness and drain.

In a large saucepan, combine with a wire whisk:
2 1/4 cups water
1 cup White Sauce Mix (p. 54)
1/4 cup dehydrated mushrooms (optional)
1 Tbsp. Onion Soup Mix (p. 34)
1 tsp. dried parsley

Bring to a boil, stirring constantly with a wire whisk. Pour over hot, cooked noodles. Sprinkle liberally with Parmesan cheese and serve immediately.

Au gratin Potatoes

In a 4-quart casserole dish, combine with a wire whisk:
2 cups water
1 cup Cheese Sauce Mix (p. 46)
1 tsp. dried parsley (optional)
1/4 tsp. dry mustard (optional)

Add 4 fresh potatoes cut in thin slices and stir
OR
2 cups dehydrated potato slices with an additional 2 cups water.

Bake uncovered at 350 degrees for 45-60 minutes.

Scalloped Potatoes

In a 4-quart baking dish combine with a wire whisk:
4 cups hot water
1 cup White Sauce Mix (p. 54)
1 Tbsp. Onion Soup Mix (p. 44)

Add 2 cups sliced dehydrated potatoes. Cover and bake at 375 degrees
for 15 minutes, then uncovered for 15 minutes. Sprinkle generously
with grated cheese just before serving (optional).

Swedish Oven Meatballs

Combine in a bowl:
1 lb. lean ground beef
2 slices fresh bread, crumbled
1 fresh egg
1 tsp. Onion Soup Mix (p. 34)
1/8 tsp. dried minced garlic or garlic powder
1/8 tsp. black pepper

Form into 20-30 small meatballs (a cookie scoop works great!). Place
on baking sheet sprayed with pan spray. Bake at 400 degrees for 15-20
minutes until browned and cooked through.

Serve with Swedish Sauce made by combining in a large pan:
2 cups water
1 cup White Sauce Mix (p. 54)
1 Tbsp. Onion Soup Mix (p. 34)

Cook until thickened, stirring with a wire whisk. Add cooked meatballs
to sauce and drain grease from baking sheet. Add 1/2 cup water to baking sheet and stir until drippings are dissolved. Add drippings carefully
to the sauce and stir gently. Add Caramelized Onions (p. 35) (optional).
Serve with baked potatoes or spoon over rice or toast.

Beef Stroganoff

Add 6 oz. wide egg noodles to two quarts boiling water. Cook 8-10 minutes until desired tenderness and drain. Brown 1/2 lb. lean hamburger or thin strips of beefsteak.

Add:
1 cup water
1/2 cup White Sauce Mix (p. 54)
1/4 cup dehydrated mushrooms (optional)
2 tsp. Onion Soup Mix (p. 34)
1/2 tsp. parsley (optional)

Cook, stirring vigorously, just until thickened. Add 1/2 cup fresh sour cream and stir until smooth. Mix lightly, pour over cooked noodles, and serve.

Quiche - The Easy Way

Mix in a blender:
2 eggs
3/4 cup water

Add and blend 1 minute:
1/4 cup Biscuit Mix (p. 12)
1 tsp. Onion Soup Mix (p. 34)
1 Tbsp. powdered milk or powdered buttermilk
1 Tbsp. dehydrated cheese
1/8 tsp. salt

Optional ingredients:
1/2 tsp. bacon, ham or pepperoni TVP
1/4 cup chopped green pepper
1/4 cup chopped ham or crumble-fried sausage
2/3 cup grated cheese

Melt 1 tsp. butter in a 7" x 7" baking dish or 8" pie tin. Sprinkle with paprika. Add egg mixture and bake at 325 degrees for 30-40 minutes.

Cream of Broccoli Soup

Steam just until fork-tender 1 cup fresh diced broccoli
OR
Follow directions on p. 55 to cook dehydrated broccoli.
Remove broccoli and add water to stock to make 3 cups.
Add:
3/4 cup White Sauce Mix (p. 54)
Cook and stir until thickened, then add steamed broccoli.

Note: Good stock for any soup can be made by simmering celery tops
and straining broth. You may want to keep a jar in your freezer to col-
lect all vegetable juices drained off before serving. This stock makes a
fuller-flavored and more nutritional soup.

Cream of Potato Soup

Boil 2 cups diced fresh potatoes. Drain off water when potatoes are tender or use 2 cups leftover cooked potatoes.

Add:
Stock or water to equal 4 cups liquid.
1 1/2 cups White Sauce Mix (p. 54)
Stir until slightly thickened.
Then Add:
1/4 cup chopped Caramelized Onions (p. 35)
1/4 cup each cooked carrots and celery pieces (optional)
2 cups cooked, diced potatoes
Garnish with bacon bits (TVP) (optional)

Clam Chowder

Make the above recipe and add one or two cans of clams. If you prefer a
thinner base, experiment with the amount of White Sauce Mix added.
For fuller flavor, you may prefer to add more powdered milk and butter.

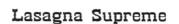

Lasagna Supreme

Prepare:
3 1/2 cups Italian Tomato Sauce (p. 52)
Add:
2 cups crumble-fried hamburger to sauce
Pour 1 cup hot water in a 7" x 12" or 9" x 11" baking dish.
Layer:
3 uncooked Lasagna noodles
1 cup cottage cheese
1 rounded cup Italian Tomato Sauce

Make three layers of noodles and sauce with sauce for top layer. Cover with foil and bake at 350 degrees for 1 hour and 20 minutes. Top with grated cheddar cheese. Melt cheese and serve.

Spaghetti Supper

Combine:
2 cups Italian Tomato Sauce (p. 52)
1 quart whole tomatoes
2 tsp. Onion Soup Mix (p. 34)
Add:
Crumble-fried hamburger or Swedish Oven Meatballs (p. 58). Serve over cooked pasta.

Cheddar Hamburger Supper

Cook 1 1/2 cups macaroni in 6 cups boiling water 8-10 minutes. Drain. In a large saucepan, brown 1 lb. lean ground beef well.
Add:
1/2 tsp. chili powder
1 tsp. Onion Soup Mix (p. 34)
Add:
3 1/2 cups warm water and stir

Sprinkle in 1 1/2 cups Cheese Sauce Mix (p. 46). Cook, stirring vigorously, until creamy and smooth. Stir in cooked macaroni and serve.

Nacho Potato Bake

In a 4-quart casserole dish, combine with wire whisk:
2 cups water
1 cup Cheese Sauce Mix (p. 46)
1/2 cup salsa or Picante' Sauce (p. 53)
Add:
4 fresh thinly-sliced potatoes and stir to cover
OR
2 cups dehydrated potato slices and 2 cups additional water.

Bake at 350 degrees for 45-60 minutes. When serving, top with extra
cheese sauce or grated cheese, as desired.

Chili - Thick and Fast

Combine in a large pan:
2 cups boiling water
1 Tbsp. chili seasoning
1 Tbsp. Onion Soup Mix (p. 34)
Add:
1/2 cup Tomato Sauce Mix (p. 52)
Stir until well blended.
Add:
2 cups cooked chili beans
1 pound crumble-fried hamburger
2 cups stewed tomatoes with juice

Bring ingredients to a simmer and serve immediately or keep it hot
in a crockpot.

Taco Salad

Cover corn chips with Chili – Thick and Fast (above). Top, as desired,
with lettuce, grated cheese, olives and peppers. Garnish with sour cream
or Dip for Chips and Veggies (p. 34).

Mexican Dinner

Combine and bring to a boil:
3 cups water
1 tsp. chili or taco seasoning
1/2 tsp. beef bouillon (soup base)
While boiling, add 1/2 cup Tomato Sauce Mix (p. 52). Dip two corn or two Flour Tortillas (p. 39) in above sauce
OR
Dip in regular tomato sauce with chili and beef seasonings. Place side by side in the bottom of a 9" x 13" pan (edges will overlap).
Add:
hot crumble-fried hamburger or Chili-Thick and Fast (p. 62)
olives
cheese

Repeat with two more layers of dipped tortillas and meat or chili topping. End with meat and grated cheese. Pour remaining sauce over the top. Cover with foil and bake at 350 degrees for 15-20 minutes until cheese melts. Cut into squares and serve immediately. Garnish with tossed salad and sour cream.

Mexican Dinner

(without baking)
Dip one flour tortilla in sauce (above) and place on a plate. Add toppings, as desired. Cover with a second dipped tortilla and a second layer of toppings. Garnish with tossed salad and sour cream. Serve immediately.

Coleslaw

Combine to make about 3 cups:
Grated cabbage, grated carrot and grated onion
Combine and boil until thickened:
1/2 cup water
2 Tbsp. white vinegar
5 Tbsp. Oriental Stir Fry Mix (p. 64). Pour sauce over grated coleslaw and chill well before serving.

ORIENTAL STIR FRY MIX

Combine:

2 cups sugar

3/4 cup cornstarch

3 1/2 Tbsp. Onion Soup Mix (p. 34)

2 tsp. onion powder

2 tsp. garlic powder

1 tsp. ground ginger

1 tsp. black pepper

MINI-MIX

Combine:

2 1/2 Tbsp. sugar

2 tsp. cornstarch

1 tsp. Onion Soup Mix (p. 34)

1/4 tsp. onion powder

1/4 tsp. ground ginger

1/4 tsp. garlic powder

1/8 tsp. black pepper

Oriental Stir Fry

Stir fry 4-5 cups of cut, thinly-sliced fresh or frozen vegetables (cabbage, onions, green peppers, carrots, green beans, mushrooms, summer squash, broccoli, and cauliflower). Cook for 5-8 minutes or until tender.

Add:

1-2 cups steamed chicken, leftover roast beef or turkey

1/2 cup water

1 Tbsp. white vinegar

1/8 cup soy sauce

Sprinkle on 1/4 cup Oriental Stir Fry Mix (above). Stir and cook for 2-3 minutes until sauce thickens.

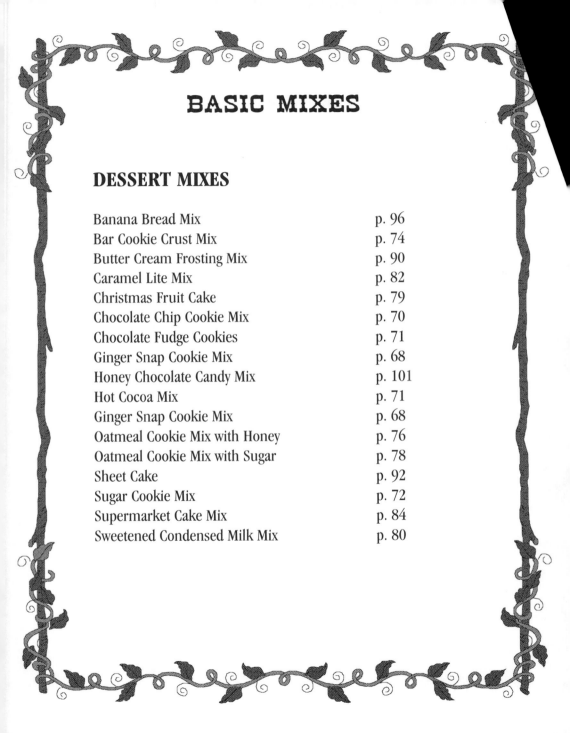

BASIC MIXES

DESSERT MIXES

BASIC COOKIE MIX

Combine:

6 cups flour

1 3/4 cups white sugar

1 1/2 cups brown sugar

1 cup dehydrated margarine or shortening

3 Tbsp. dehydrated whole eggs

2 tsp. salt

1 1/4 tsp. baking soda

MINI-MIX

Combine:

1 cup flour

1/3 cup white sugar

1/4 cup brown sugar

3 Tbsp. dehydrated margarine or shortening

1/2 Tbsp. dehydrated whole egg

1/4 tsp. salt

1/8 tsp. baking soda

Pineapple Macaroons

Combine:

1 1/2 cups Basic Cookie Mix (above)

2/3 cup shredded coconut

1/2 cup crushed pineapple with juice

1/2 cup chopped nuts

Mixture seems dry at first. Continue stirring until all ingredients are moist. Drop dough by teaspoonsful onto lightly greased baking sheets. Bake at 350 degrees for 12-15 minutes until edges are golden brown. Glaze while hot with Lemon Butter Cream Glaze Mix (p. 91).

Peanut Butter Cookies

Combine:
1 cup Basic Cookie Mix (p. 66)
1/8 cup brown sugar
1/4 cup chunky-style peanut butter
1/4 cup water
OR
1 cup Basic Cookie Mix (p. 66)
1/4 cup brown sugar
1/2 cup dehydrated peanut butter
1/2 to 2/3 cup water

Shape into 1" balls and place on a greased cookie sheet. Flatten with fork tines dipped in sugar. Bake at 375 degrees for 10-12 minutes.

Ginger Snap Cookies

Combine:
1 1/4 cups Basic Cookie Mix (p. 66)
1/2 tsp. ginger
1/2 tsp. cinnamon
1/2 tsp. allspice

Add:
1/4 cup molasses
3 Tbsp. water

Drop by half teaspoonsful on greased cookie sheet. Flatten with the bottom of a glass dipped in sugar. Bake at 350 degrees for 10-12 minutes.

Note: If you are a Ginger Snap lover, you may want the convenience of the Ginger Snap Cookie Mix found on page 68.

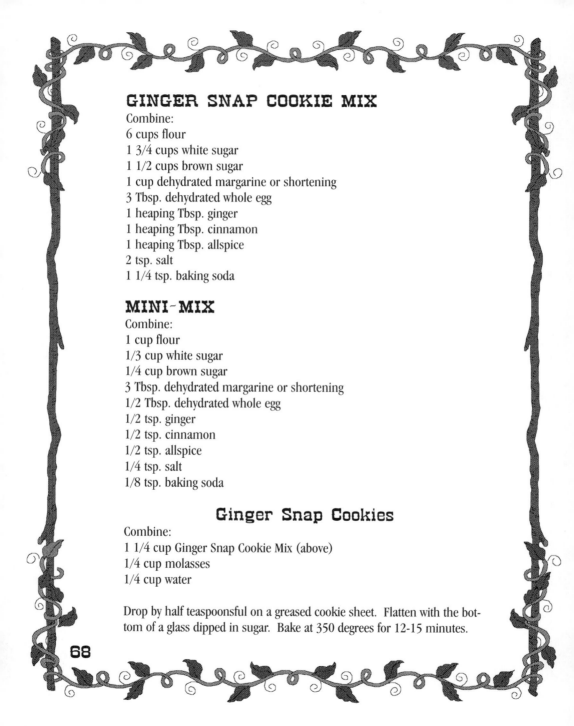

GINGER SNAP COOKIE MIX

Combine:

6 cups flour

1 3/4 cups white sugar

1 1/2 cups brown sugar

1 cup dehydrated margarine or shortening

3 Tbsp. dehydrated whole egg

1 heaping Tbsp. ginger

1 heaping Tbsp. cinnamon

1 heaping Tbsp. allspice

2 tsp. salt

1 1/4 tsp. baking soda

MINI-MIX

Combine:

1 cup flour

1/3 cup white sugar

1/4 cup brown sugar

3 Tbsp. dehydrated margarine or shortening

1/2 Tbsp. dehydrated whole egg

1/2 tsp. ginger

1/2 tsp. cinnamon

1/2 tsp. allspice

1/4 tsp. salt

1/8 tsp. baking soda

Ginger Snap Cookies

Combine:

1 1/4 cup Ginger Snap Cookie Mix (above)

1/4 cup molasses

1/4 cup water

Drop by half teaspoonsful on a greased cookie sheet. Flatten with the bottom of a glass dipped in sugar. Bake at 350 degrees for 12-15 minutes.

CRUMBLE TOPPING MIX

Combine:

2 cups brown sugar
1 cup chopped nuts
3/4 cup dehydrated margarine or butter
1/2 cup Biscuit Mix (p. 12)
1 1/2 Tbsp. cinnamon

MINI-MIX

Combine:

1/2 cup brown sugar
1/4 cup chopped nuts
3 Tbsp. dehydrated margarine or butter
2 Tbsp. Biscuit Mix (p. 12)
1 tsp. cinnamon

Use with the following recipes:

Breakfast Cake	p. 19
Fruit Breakfast Pizza	p. 14
Muffins	p. 32
Cinnamon Rolls	p. 27
Heavenly Orange Rolls	p. 27

Note: The butter in this topping mix gives it a rich taste and it browns well. Use it generously as a topping for an added touch of flavor to cookies and other baked desserts.

CHOCOLATE CHIP COOKIE MIX

Combine:
5 1/3 cups flour
1 1/3 cups ground oatmeal*
2 cups brown sugar
2 cups white sugar
2 cups dehydrated margarine
1/4 cup dehydrated whole eggs
2 tsp. baking powder
2 tsp. baking soda
1 tsp. salt
1/2 tsp. powdered vanilla

MINI-MIX

Combine:
1 1/3 cups flour
1/3 cup ground oatmeal*
1/2 cup brown sugar
1/2 cup white sugar
1/2 cup dehydrated margarine
1 Tbsp. dehydrated whole eggs
1/2 tsp. baking powder
1/2 tsp. baking soda
1/4 tsp. salt
1/16 tsp. powdered vanilla

Chocolate Chip Cookies

Combine:
2 cups Chocolate Chip Cookie Mix (above)
1/3 cup water
1/2 cup chocolate chips
1/4 cup chopped nuts

Drop by teaspoonsful or cookie scoop on sprayed or greased sheet. For crisper cookies, flatten with a glass dipped in sugar before baking. Bake at 375 degrees for 10-12 minutes.

Note: Ground oatmeal flour keeps the cookie moist and improves the texture. Rolled oats can be ground in a wheat grinder or ground in a blender.

70

Chocolate Fudge Cookies

Combine:
2 cups Chocolate Chip Cookie Mix (p. 70)
1/4 cup cooking cocoa
1/2 cup chocolate chips
1/4 cup chopped nuts
Add:
1/3 cup water

Drop by teaspoonsful on a sprayed or greased cookie sheet. Bake at 375 degrees for 10-12 minutes.

HOT COCOA MIX

Combine:
4 1/2 cups regular powdered milk or 9 cups instant powdered milk
1 cup sugar
1/2 cup cocoa

MINI-MIX

Combine:
2 Tbsp. regular powdered milk or 1/4 cup instant powdered milk
1/2 tsp. cocoa
1 tsp. sugar

Hot Chocolate

Combine in quart jar, cover and shake hard, or mix on low in a blender:
1/3 cup Hot Cocoa Mix made with regular milk, or
2/3 cup Hot Cocoa Mix made with instant milk
1 cup hottest tap water

Note: This mix has no thickeners or preservatives and it tastes better than commercial cocoa mixes!

SUGAR COOKIE MIX

Combine:

6 cups flour

3 cups sugar

1 1/2 cups dehydrated butter

1 1/2 tsp. baking powder

2 tsp. cream of tartar (a must)

1 1/2 tsp. salt

1 tsp. powdered vanilla

MINI-MIX

Combine:

2 cups flour

1 cup sugar

1/2 cup dehydrated butter

1/2 tsp. baking powder

1/2 tsp. cream of tartar (a must)

1/2 tsp. salt

1/8 tsp. powdered vanilla

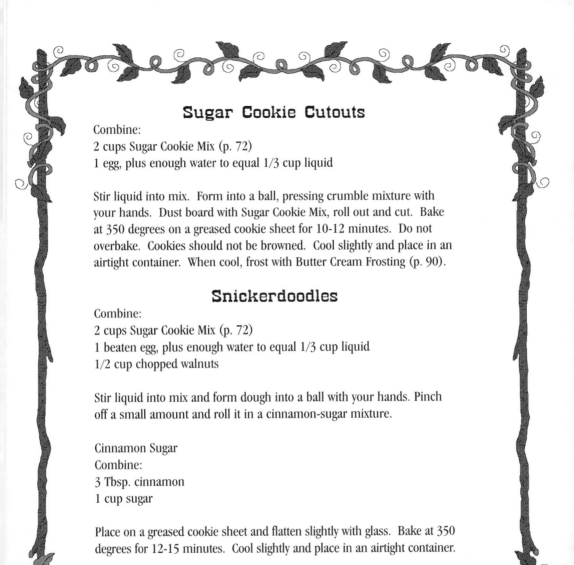

Sugar Cookie Cutouts

Combine:

2 cups Sugar Cookie Mix (p. 72)

1 egg, plus enough water to equal 1/3 cup liquid

Stir liquid into mix. Form into a ball, pressing crumble mixture with your hands. Dust board with Sugar Cookie Mix, roll out and cut. Bake at 350 degrees on a greased cookie sheet for 10-12 minutes. Do not overbake. Cookies should not be browned. Cool slightly and place in an airtight container. When cool, frost with Butter Cream Frosting (p. 90).

Snickerdoodles

Combine:

2 cups Sugar Cookie Mix (p. 72)

1 beaten egg, plus enough water to equal 1/3 cup liquid

1/2 cup chopped walnuts

Stir liquid into mix and form dough into a ball with your hands. Pinch off a small amount and roll it in a cinnamon-sugar mixture.

Cinnamon Sugar
Combine:
3 Tbsp. cinnamon
1 cup sugar

Place on a greased cookie sheet and flatten slightly with glass. Bake at 350 degrees for 12-15 minutes. Cool slightly and place in an airtight container.

BAR COOKIE CRUST MIX

Combine:
4 cups rolled oats
4 cups brown sugar
3 1/2 cups whole wheat or white flour
1 Tbsp. baking soda
1/2 Tbsp. cream of tartar
1 tsp. salt

MINI-MIX

Combine:
1 1/4 cups rolled oats
1 1/4 cups brown sugar
1 cup whole wheat or white flour
1 tsp. baking soda
1/2 tsp. cream of tartar
1/4 tsp. salt

Bar Cookies

Combine:
3 cups Bar Cookie Crust Mix (above)
1 cube (1/2 cup) softened or melted table margarine

To make the crust, flour your fingers and pat half of the crust mixture in a greased 9" x 9" square pan. Reserve the other half of the mixture as a topping crust.

Cover with a filling:
Date Bar Cookie Filling   p. 75
Mincemeat Bar Cookie Filling   p. 75
Apple Bar Cookie Filling   p. 75
Any canned pie filling works great

Crumble remaining crust mixture over the top. Bake at 350 degrees for 20 minutes. Cut in 2"-3" squares and serve hot with ice cream or whipped cream.

Date Bar Cookie Filling

Combine:
2 cups chopped dates
2 Tbsp. brown sugar
Juice of half of a lemon or 2 Tbsp. lemon concentrate
1 cup water

Combine all ingredients in a saucepan. Cook, stirring constantly, for 5 minutes. Use with Bar Cookie Crust (p. 74) in a 9" x 9" pan.

Apple Bar Cookie Filling

Combine:
3 cups cooked sliced apples
OR
3 cups thick reconstituted applesauce
1/4 cup brown sugar
1/2 tsp. cinnamon

Combine and use with Bar Cookie Crust (p. 74). Makes filling for 9" x 9" pan.

Mincemeat Bar Cookie Filling

3 cups Mincemeat (p. 79)

Drain liquid from mincemeat and use with Bar Cookie Crust (p. 74). Makes filling for 9" x 9" pan. This tastes even better the second day!

Note: Any pie filling works well with this crust!

OATMEAL COOKIE MIX WITH HONEY

Combine:

9 cups whole wheat flour

1 1/2 cups dehydrated applesauce (optional), see p. 77

1/4 cup cinnamon

2 Tbsp. baking powder

1 Tbsp. baking soda

MINI-MIX

Combine:

3 cups whole wheat flour

1/2 cup dehydrated applesauce (optional), see p. 77

4 tsp. cinnamon

2 tsp. baking powder

1 tsp. baking soda

Note: Four Oatmeal Cookie Mixes will fill a 30-pound container (a Maxi-Mix!)

Oatmeal Honey Cookies

Boil 1 cup raisins in 1 1/2 cups water and cool.

Combine:
4 eggs
1 1/2 cups soft honey
1 cup raisin water (add water, if needed, to make 1 cup)

Add:
4 cups Oatmeal Cookie Mix (for Oatmeal Honey Cookies) (p. 76)
2 cups regular or instant rolled oats
1 cup cooked raisins
1/2 cup chopped walnuts

Bake on greased cookie sheet at 350 degrees for 15-17 minutes. These cookies store well in the freezer.

Options:

When making the mix (p. 76) WITHOUT dehydrated applesauce, add 1/3 cup canned applesauce to eggs and honey. Use 1/2 cup raisin water and 3 1/2 cups Oatmeal Cookie Mix (for Oatmeal Honey Cookies) (p. 76).

For low-fat cookies, substitute equal amounts of dehydrated shortening or butter for the dehydrated applesauce in the mix (p. 76).

77

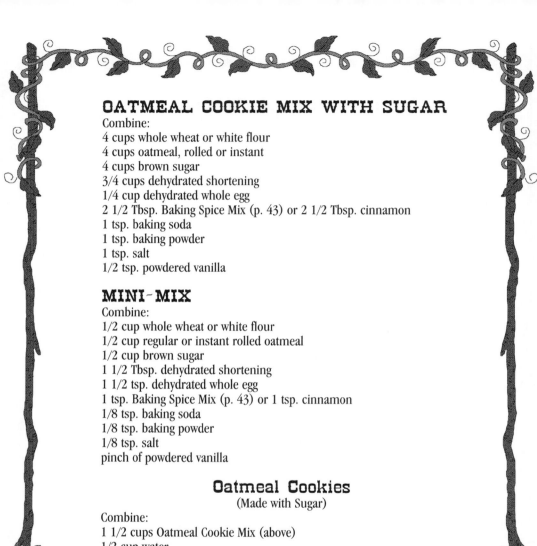

OATMEAL COOKIE MIX WITH SUGAR

Combine:

4 cups whole wheat or white flour
4 cups oatmeal, rolled or instant
4 cups brown sugar
3/4 cups dehydrated shortening
1/4 cup dehydrated whole egg
2 1/2 Tbsp. Baking Spice Mix (p. 43) or 2 1/2 Tbsp. cinnamon
1 tsp. baking soda
1 tsp. baking powder
1 tsp. salt
1/2 tsp. powdered vanilla

MINI-MIX

Combine:

1/2 cup whole wheat or white flour
1/2 cup regular or instant rolled oatmeal
1/2 cup brown sugar
1 1/2 Tbsp. dehydrated shortening
1 1/2 tsp. dehydrated whole egg
1 tsp. Baking Spice Mix (p. 43) or 1 tsp. cinnamon
1/8 tsp. baking soda
1/8 tsp. baking powder
1/8 tsp. salt
pinch of powdered vanilla

Oatmeal Cookies
(Made with Sugar)

Combine:

1 1/2 cups Oatmeal Cookie Mix (above)
1/2 cup water
3/4 cup raisins or chocolate chips
1/3 cup chopped nuts

Drop by teaspoonful or cookie scoop onto a greased cookie sheet.
Flatten with a glass dipped in cinnamon sugar (p. 73). Bake at 350
degrees for 15 minutes.

Mincemeat

Combine and let sit 5 minutes:
2 cups raisins
1/2 cup dehydrated applesauce
2 cups cold water

Bring to a boil, lower heat, cover and cook until liquid is absorbed
(about 10 minutes).
Stir in:
1/2 cup corn syrup
1 Tbsp. molasses
2 tsp. vinegar
1/2 tsp. cloves

Cover and refrigerate several hours or overnight to blend flavors.

Christmas Fruit Cake

Combine:
2 1/2 cups whole wheat flour
1 1/8 cups Sweetened Condensed Milk Mix (p. 80)
2 Tbsp. dehydrated whole egg
1 tsp. baking soda
Add and mix well:
2/3 cup hot tap water
1 recipe Mincemeat (above) or 28 oz. bottled mincemeat
Add and stir just until moistened:
2 cups candied fruit
1 cup walnuts
1 cup dates (optional)

Grease and flour three 3 1/2" x 6 1/2" loaf pans.
or
one 9" tube or Bundt pan. Grease bottom and sides of loaf pans or line bot-
toms with brown paper. Grease both sides of the paper for easier removal.
Bake at 325 degrees for 1-1 1/2 hours until toothpick comes out clean.

SWEETENED CONDENSED MILK MIX

Combine:

6 cups sugar

1 1/2 cups dehydrated margarine or butter

6 cups powdered milk

MINI-MIX

Combine:

1/2 cup sugar

1/8 cup dehydrated margarine or butter

1/2 cup powdered milk

This recipe works equally well with either instant
or regular powdered milk!

Sweetened Condensed Milk

(may be used with any sweetened condensed milk recipe)

Start with 1/4 cup very hot water in a blender. While blender is running,
gradually add 1 1/8 cups Sweetened Condensed Milk Mix (above).
Process until smooth. Makes 14 oz.

Swedish Rice Pudding

Combine:
1/2 cup prepared Sweetened Condensed Milk (p. 80)
1 1/2 to 2 cups hot cooked rice

Garnish with 1/2-1 tsp. cinnamon sugar (p. 73). Serve with milk, whipped cream or ice cream.

Lemon Cream Cheese Pie

Prepare 1 full recipe Bar Cookie Crust Mix (p. 74) for pie crust. Stir and pat out all of crust mixture into a greased 9" x 13" pan. Bake at 350 degrees for 6-8 minutes.

Filling:
Beat one 8-oz. package cream cheese until light and fluffy.

Combine in sauce pan:
1/3 cup boiling water
1/3 cup lemon juice
1/2 tsp. powdered vanilla

Add and Mix:
2 1/4 cups Sweetened Condensed Milk Mix (p. 80).

Combine:
COOLED lemon mixture with whipped cream cheese. Beat mixture until creamy and smooth. Fold in 2 cups whipped cream or non-dairy substitute.

Spread lemon cheese pie filling over COOLED prepared crust. Refrigerate 2-3 hours. Top with cherry pie filling. Sprinkle with slivered almonds.

Caramel Popcorn

Mix together in a pan:
1 cup corn syrup
1/2 cup boiling water

Stir until corn syrup dissolves.

Add to boiling liquid:
1 1/8 cups Sweetened Condensed Milk Mix (p. 80)
2 cups brown sugar
1/2 cup dehydrated butter or margarine
1/4 tsp. powdered vanilla

Lower heat and cook to soft ball stage (234-238 degrees) (it cooks up fast!). Pour hot mixture over 1 gallon popped popcorn. Add peanuts and serve like Cracker Jacks or make into popcorn balls.

CARAMEL LITE MIX

4 cups brown sugar
2 2/3 cups dehydrated margarine or butter
4 cups powdered milk
1/4 tsp. powdered vanilla

MINI-MIX

1/2 cup brown sugar
1/2 cup dehydrated margarine or butter
1/3 cup powdered milk
pinch of powdered vanilla

Use this caramel mix with the recipes on page 83.

Caramel Lite Sauce
(Great as an ice cream topping or for popcorn treats)

Mix together and bring to a boil:
1/2 cup corn syrup or light clover honey
1/4 cup hot water

Add 1 1/3 cups Caramel Lite Mix (p. 82) to boiling liquid. Lower heat and cook until mixture reaches soft ball stage (234-238 degrees).

Note: If sauce gets too thick in the refrigerator, add a little hot water before serving.

Caramel Honey Popcorn Balls

Make Caramel Lite Sauce (above).
Add chopped pecans or roasted peanuts (optional).
Pour hot caramel sauce over 1 gallon popped popcorn. With buttered hands, form mixture into popcorn balls.

Caramel Honey Popcorn Cake

Follow above recipe and press into a buttered tube or bundt pan. Turn out immediately onto a plate. Decorate top with sliced gumdrops or other candies. Slice to serve.

SUPERMARKET CAKE MIX

Combine:
7 cups flour
5 1/4 cups sugar
1 3/4 cups dehydrated shortening
1/3 rounded cup powdered milk
3 Tbsp. baking powder
2 1/2 tsp. powdered vanilla
2 scant tsp. salt

MINI-MIX

Combine:
1 cup flour
3/4 cup sugar
1/4 cup dehydrated shortening
1 Tbsp. powdered milk
1 1/4 tsp. baking powder
1/4 tsp. powdered vanilla
1/4 tsp. salt

Note: If fresh eggs are not available, for each cup of mix, add 1 Tbsp. dehydrated whole egg or dehydrated egg white, plus 3 additional Tbsp. water to each recipe.

Use this mix for the following recipes:

Yellow Cake	Marble Cake
Orange Cake	Chocolate Cake
Applesauce Spice Cake	Sponge Cake or Shortcake

Yellow Cake

For 8" layer cake combine:
2 cups Supermarket Cake Mix (p. 84)
1 large fresh egg
1/2 cup, plus 2 Tbsp. water
1 tsp. liquid vanilla

For 9" layer cake combine:
2 1/2 cups Supermarket Cake Mix (p. 84)
1 large fresh egg
3/4 cup water
1 tsp. liquid vanilla

Beat on medium speed for two minutes. Bake at 350 degrees in 8" or 9" greased and floured pan for approximately 30 minutes, cupcakes for approximately 20-25 minutes, or a 9" x 13" pan (double the 9" recipe) for approximately 40 minutes.

Shortcake or Sponge Cake

Combine:
2 cups Supermarket Cake Mix (p. 84)
2 tsp. dehydrated egg white or whole egg (optional)
1/2 cup, plus 2 Tbsp. water
1 tsp. liquid vanilla

Bake in an 8" greased and floured pan at 350 degrees for 30 minutes. Top with berries or fresh peaches and whipped cream or ice cream.

Marble Cake

Prepare an 8" or 9" Yellow Cake (p. 85). Pour all but half cup of the batter into greased and floured cake pan. Add 2 Tbsp. cocoa to remaining batter and mix well. Drop chocolate batter by teaspoonsful onto the Yellow Cake batter. Cut through batter with 2-3 long strokes with a knife. Bake at 350 degrees for approximately 30 minutes.

Orange Cake

Mix batter according to directions for an 8" or 9" Yellow Cake (p. 85).

Add:
1/2 tsp. grated orange peel or dehydrated orange peel.

Tip: If you grate and freeze lemon and orange peelings as you use the fruit, it's very convenient when cooking!

Add:
1/2 tsp. powdered orange flavoring

Bake at 350 degrees for approximately 30 minutes. Frost with Orange Butter Cream Frosting (p. 91).

Applesauce Spice Cake

Combine in bowl and let sit for 3-5 minutes:
1/4 cup dehydrated applesauce
1 cup water
Add:
1 egg
2 cups Supermarket Cake Mix (p. 84)
1/3 cup raisins
2 scant tsp. Baking Spice Mix (p. 43)

Bake at 350 degrees in a 9" x 9" pan for 35-40 minutes. Cool and frost with Banana Butter Cream Frosting (p. 91).

German Chocolate Cake

Combine:
2 1/2 cups Supermarket Cake Mix (p. 84)
1/4 cup baking cocoa
1/4 cup sugar

Add:
1 large fresh egg
3/4 cup water

Beat on medium speed for two minutes. Bake at 350 degrees in a 9"
greased and floured pan for 35-40 minutes. When done, a toothpick will
come out clean from the middle of the cake. Frost with German
Chocolate Frosting (below).

German Chocolate Frosting
(Frosts one 9" layer cake)

Cook and stir until sugar melts (about 1-2 minutes):
1/2 cup cooked Frosting Mix (p. 88)
1/8 cup water

Add:
1/2 cup coconut
1/2 cup chopped nuts

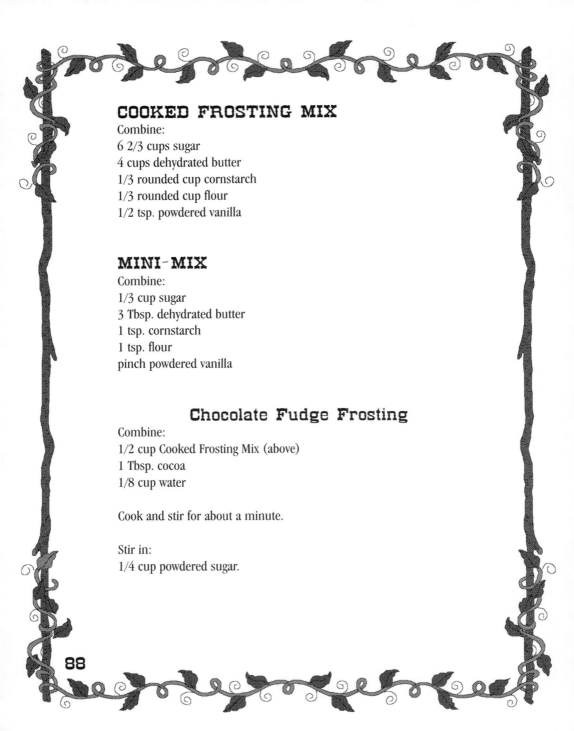

COOKED FROSTING MIX

Combine:

6 2/3 cups sugar

4 cups dehydrated butter

1/3 rounded cup cornstarch

1/3 rounded cup flour

1/2 tsp. powdered vanilla

MINI-MIX

Combine:

1/3 cup sugar

3 Tbsp. dehydrated butter

1 tsp. cornstarch

1 tsp. flour

pinch powdered vanilla

Chocolate Fudge Frosting

Combine:

1/2 cup Cooked Frosting Mix (above)

1 Tbsp. cocoa

1/8 cup water

Cook and stir for about a minute.

Stir in:

1/4 cup powdered sugar.

DEVILS FOOD WHOLE WHEAT CAKE MIX

Combine:
6 cups whole wheat flour
4 cups sugar
1 1/2 cups baking cocoa
1 1/4 cups dehydrated shortening
1/4 cup powdered milk
1/4 cup dehydrated whole eggs
2 Tbsp. baking soda
2 1/2 tsp. powdered vanilla
1 1/2 tsp. salt

MINI-MIX

Combine:
1 1/2 cups whole wheat flour
1 cup sugar
1/3 cup baking cocoa
1/4 cup dehydrated shortening
2 Tbsp. powdered milk
2 Tbsp. dehydrated whole eggs
1 1/2 tsp. baking soda
1/4 tsp. powdered vanilla
1/8 tsp. salt

Devils Food Whole Wheat Cake

Combine:
2 1/2 cups Devils Food Whole Wheat Cake Mix (above)
1 1/4 cups water

Beat two minutes. Bake at 350 degrees in a greased and floured 9" pan
for 35 minutes.

Note: For a special taste and texture, try:
2 1/2 cups Devils Food Whole Wheat Cake Mix (above)
3/4 cup water
1/2 cup buttermilk

Bake in a greased and floured 9" cake pan at 350 degrees for 40 minutes.

BUTTER CREAM FROSTING MIX

Combine:

8 cups powdered sugar

1 1/2 cups dehydrated margarine or butter

1 cup cornstarch

1/2 tsp. powdered vanilla

MINI-MIX

Combine:

2 cups powdered sugar

1/3 cup margarine or butter

1/4 cup cornstarch

pinch powdered vanilla

Butter Cream Frosting
(for 9" layer cake)

Combine:

1 1/2 cups Butter Cream Frosting Mix (above)

1 Tbsp. water, plus one tsp. water

Stir until mixture is creamy (approx. one minute).

For a glaze, thin frosting by adding more water. Spread or drizzle over cake while it is still warm.

Chocolate Butter Cream Frosting
(for 9" layer cake)

Follow the recipe for Butter Cream Frosting (above). Add 2 Tablespoons cooking cocoa. Stir until mixture is creamy. Add 1/4 tsp. more water, if needed.

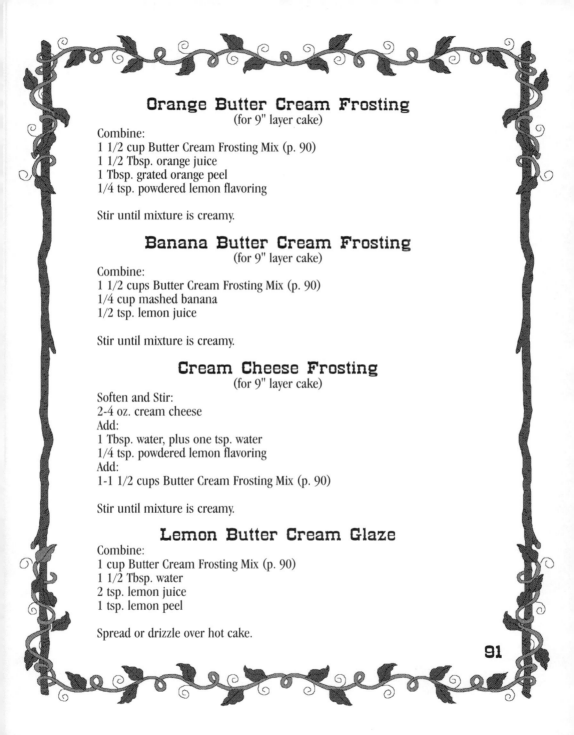

Orange Butter Cream Frosting
(for 9" layer cake)

Combine:
1 1/2 cup Butter Cream Frosting Mix (p. 90)
1 1/2 Tbsp. orange juice
1 Tbsp. grated orange peel
1/4 tsp. powdered lemon flavoring

Stir until mixture is creamy.

Banana Butter Cream Frosting
(for 9" layer cake)

Combine:
1 1/2 cups Butter Cream Frosting Mix (p. 90)
1/4 cup mashed banana
1/2 tsp. lemon juice

Stir until mixture is creamy.

Cream Cheese Frosting
(for 9" layer cake)

Soften and Stir:
2-4 oz. cream cheese
Add:
1 Tbsp. water, plus one tsp. water
1/4 tsp. powdered lemon flavoring
Add:
1-1 1/2 cups Butter Cream Frosting Mix (p. 90)

Stir until mixture is creamy.

Lemon Butter Cream Glaze

Combine:
1 cup Butter Cream Frosting Mix (p. 90)
1 1/2 Tbsp. water
2 tsp. lemon juice
1 tsp. lemon peel

Spread or drizzle over hot cake.

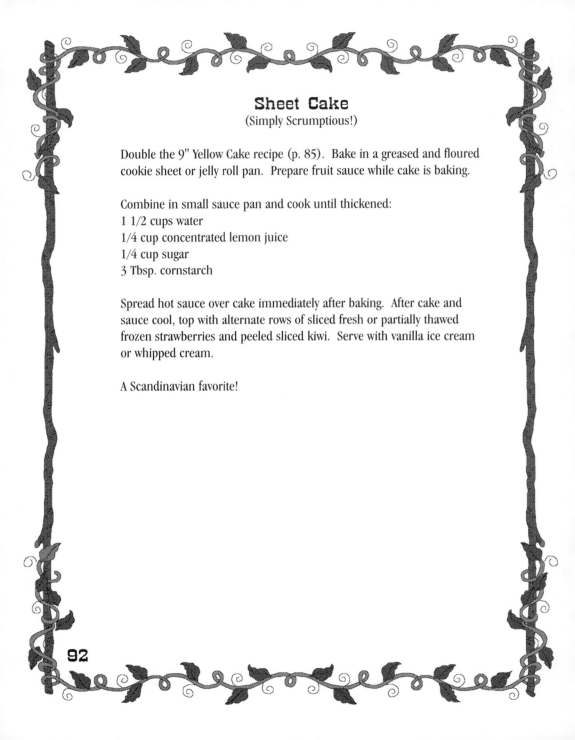

Sheet Cake
(Simply Scrumptious!)

Double the 9" Yellow Cake recipe (p. 85). Bake in a greased and floured cookie sheet or jelly roll pan. Prepare fruit sauce while cake is baking.

Combine in small sauce pan and cook until thickened:
1 1/2 cups water
1/4 cup concentrated lemon juice
1/4 cup sugar
3 Tbsp. cornstarch

Spread hot sauce over cake immediately after baking. After cake and sauce cool, top with alternate rows of sliced fresh or partially thawed frozen strawberries and peeled sliced kiwi. Serve with vanilla ice cream or whipped cream.

A Scandinavian favorite!

BROWNIE MIX

Combine:

5 cups sugar
3 1/3 cups flour
1 2/3 cups ground oatmeal (p. 70)
1 1/4 cups cooking cocoa
1/2 rounded cup dehydrated shortening or margarine
1/3 cup dehydrated egg white or whole egg
1 Tbsp. baking powder
1 1/4 tsp. salt
1/2 rounded tsp. cream of tartar
1/2 tsp. powdered vanilla
1/4 rounded tsp. baking soda

MINI-MIX

Combine:

1 cup sugar
2/3 cup flour
1/3 cup ground oatmeal (p. 70)
1/4 cup cocoa
2 Tbsp. dehydrated shortening or margarine
1 Tbsp. dehydrated egg white or whole egg
1/2 tsp. baking powder
1/4 tsp. salt
1/8 tsp. cream of tartar
1/16 tsp. powdered vanilla
1/16 tsp. baking soda

Brownies

Combine:
2 cups Brownie Mix (p. 93)
1/2 cup water
1/2 cup chopped walnuts

Bake at 350 degrees for 35 minutes in a greased and floured 8" x 8" pan. Cool slightly. Frost with Chocolate Butter Cream Frosting (p. 90).

Note: If dehydrated eggs are unavailable, make the mix without it using 2 cups Brownie Mix (p. 95), 2 beaten eggs, and 2 Tbsp. water. Bake as above.

Brownie Pudding

Spread Brownie batter (above) in an 8" x 8" pan.

Combine:
2 Tbsp. cocoa
1/3 cup sugar
1 1/2 cups hottest tap water

Dissolve cocoa and sugar in the water. Pour on top of the brownie batter. Bake at 350 degrees for 30 minutes. Serve hot or cold.

Fudge Sauce

1 cup Brownie Mix (p. 93)
1/4 tsp. powdered vanilla
1 cup hot water (add a little more if cooked sauce is too thick)

Bring mixture to a boil, stirring constantly, until thick and smooth.

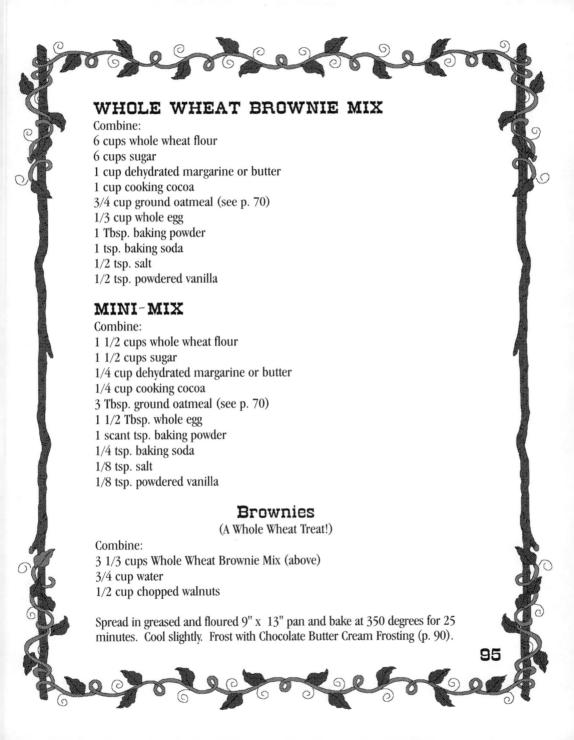

WHOLE WHEAT BROWNIE MIX

Combine:
6 cups whole wheat flour
6 cups sugar
1 cup dehydrated margarine or butter
1 cup cooking cocoa
3/4 cup ground oatmeal (see p. 70)
1/3 cup whole egg
1 Tbsp. baking powder
1 tsp. baking soda
1/2 tsp. salt
1/2 tsp. powdered vanilla

MINI-MIX

Combine:
1 1/2 cups whole wheat flour
1 1/2 cups sugar
1/4 cup dehydrated margarine or butter
1/4 cup cooking cocoa
3 Tbsp. ground oatmeal (see p. 70)
1 1/2 Tbsp. whole egg
1 scant tsp. baking powder
1/4 tsp. baking soda
1/8 tsp. salt
1/8 tsp. powdered vanilla

Brownies
(A Whole Wheat Treat!)

Combine:
3 1/3 cups Whole Wheat Brownie Mix (above)
3/4 cup water
1/2 cup chopped walnuts

Spread in greased and floured 9" x 13" pan and bake at 350 degrees for 25 minutes. Cool slightly. Frost with Chocolate Butter Cream Frosting (p. 90).

BANANA BREAD MIX

Combine:

6 3/4 cups whole wheat or white flour

2 cups white sugar

2 cups brown sugar

2 1/4 cups dehydrated margarine or butter

1 cup powdered milk

1 cup dehydrated whole egg

3 Tbsp. baking powder

1 scant Tbsp. salt

1 scant Tbsp. baking soda

2 tsp. powdered vanilla

1 1/2 tsp. powdered butterscotch flavoring

MINI-MIX

Combine:

1 scant cup flour

1/3 cup white sugar

1/3 cup brown sugar

1/3 cup dehydrated margarine or butter

1 Tbsp. powdered milk

1 Tbsp. dehydrated whole egg

1 1/4 tsp. baking powder

1/2 tsp. salt

1/16 tsp. powdered vanilla

pinch of powdered butterscotch flavoring

Banana Bread

Combine:
1 mashed ripe banana
1/2 cup water
1 fresh egg

Add:
1 1/2 cups Banana Bread Mix (p. 96)
1/2 cup nuts

Pour into a greased, floured 5 1/2" x 2 1/2" loaf pan. Bake at 350 degrees for approximately 1 hour.

Raisin Loaf

Combine:
2 cups Banana Bread Mix (p. 96)
1/2 cup raisins
1/4 cup nuts
1 1/2 Tbsp. Baking Spice Mix (p. 43)
3/4 cup crushed pineapple with juice

Pour into a greased and floured 5 1/2" x 2 1/2" loaf pan. Bake at 350 degrees for approximately 1 hour.

Note: All fruit breads should sit 10 minutes before turning out of the pan.

Date-Orange Bread

Combine:
1 2/3 cups Banana Bread Mix (p. 96)
1/2 cup dates
1 tsp. cinnamon
1/2 tsp. powdered orange flavoring
1 Tbsp. grated orange peel
pulp and juice of 1 orange and water to equal 1 cup
or
1 rounded Tbsp. frozen orange juice in 1 scant cup water

Pour into greased and floured 5 1/2" x 2 1/2" loaf pan. Bake at 350 degrees for approximately 1 hour.

Zucchini Lemon Bread

Combine:
2 cups Banana Bread Mix (p. 96)
1/2 cup grated zucchini
1/2 cup chopped nuts
1/4 cup brown sugar
1/4 cup, plus 2 Tbsp. water
1 Tbsp. grated lemon peel
1/2 tsp. powdered lemon flavoring
1 Tbsp. Baking Spice Mix (p. 43) or cinnamon

Pour into greased and floured 5 1/2" x 2 1/2" loaf pan. Bake at 350 degrees for approximately 1 hour.

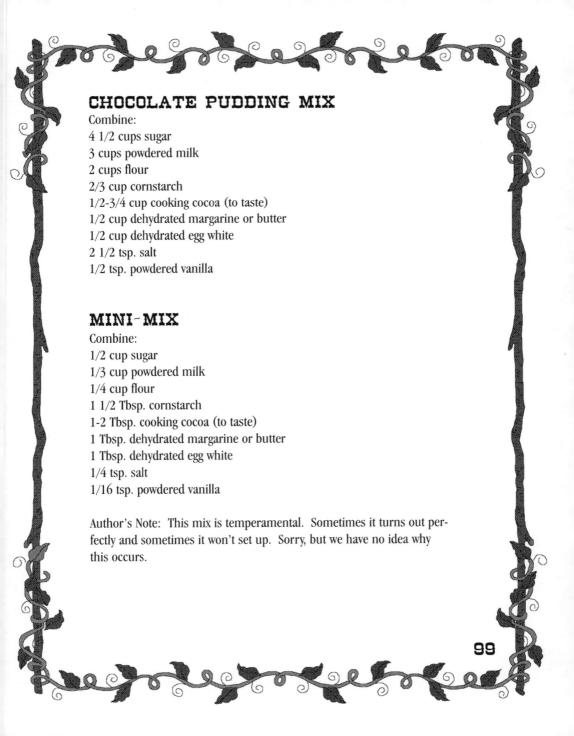

CHOCOLATE PUDDING MIX

Combine:

4 1/2 cups sugar
3 cups powdered milk
2 cups flour
2/3 cup cornstarch
1/2-3/4 cup cooking cocoa (to taste)
1/2 cup dehydrated margarine or butter
1/2 cup dehydrated egg white
2 1/2 tsp. salt
1/2 tsp. powdered vanilla

MINI-MIX

Combine:

1/2 cup sugar
1/3 cup powdered milk
1/4 cup flour
1 1/2 Tbsp. cornstarch
1-2 Tbsp. cooking cocoa (to taste)
1 Tbsp. dehydrated margarine or butter
1 Tbsp. dehydrated egg white
1/4 tsp. salt
1/16 tsp. powdered vanilla

Author's Note: This mix is temperamental. Sometimes it turns out perfectly and sometimes it won't set up. Sorry, but we have no idea why this occurs.

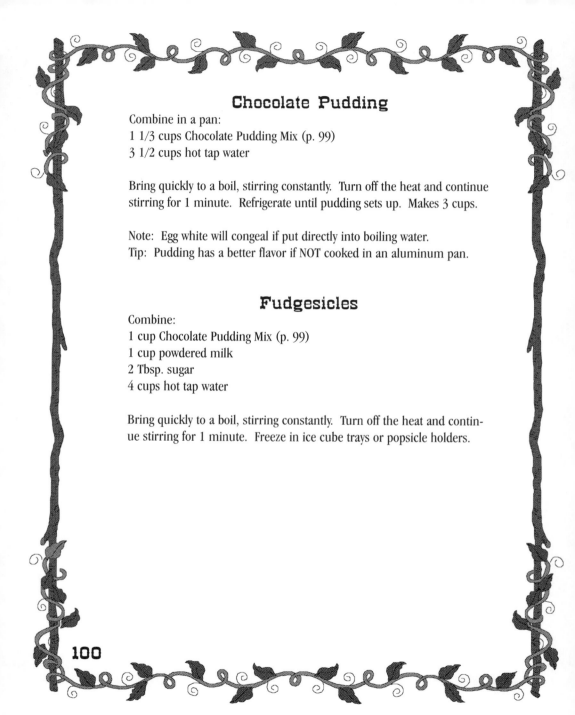

Chocolate Pudding

Combine in a pan:
1 1/3 cups Chocolate Pudding Mix (p. 99)
3 1/2 cups hot tap water

Bring quickly to a boil, stirring constantly. Turn off the heat and continue stirring for 1 minute. Refrigerate until pudding sets up. Makes 3 cups.

Note: Egg white will congeal if put directly into boiling water.
Tip: Pudding has a better flavor if NOT cooked in an aluminum pan.

Fudgesicles

Combine:
1 cup Chocolate Pudding Mix (p. 99)
1 cup powdered milk
2 Tbsp. sugar
4 cups hot tap water

Bring quickly to a boil, stirring constantly. Turn off the heat and continue stirring for 1 minute. Freeze in ice cube trays or popsicle holders.

HONEY CHOCOLATE CANDY MIX

Combine:

3 1/3 cups powdered milk

1/2 cup cooking cocoa (3/4 cup for dark chocolate lovers)

1 1/4 tsp. powdered vanilla

MINI-MIX

Combine:

1/3 cup powdered milk

2 Tbsp. cooking cocoa (3 Tbsp. for dark chocolate lovers)

1/8 tsp. powdered vanilla

Honey Chocolate Candy

Bring 1/2 cup honey to a boil and boil for 1 minute, 15 seconds. Remove from heat and add half cup Honey Chocolate Candy Mix (above). Blend with a wire whisk and let cool in the pan for 1-2 minutes. Pour candy onto a buttered pie plate or dish. Let it cool just long enough to be able to handle it. Butter your hands and, while candy is still warm, roll it to approximately the size of your little finger and coil it (not touching sides) on a buttered plate. For a soft candy (like a Tootsie Roll), cut into 1" pieces. Wrap individual pieces in waxed paper. For hard candy, cut into bite-sized pieces and dust with powdered sugar. Store in a covered candy dish.

HONEY BUTTERSCOTCH CANDY MIX

Combine:

3 1/3 cups powdered milk

1/2 cup dehydrated butter or margarine

1 tsp. powdered butterscotch flavoring

MINI-MIX

Combine:

1/3 cup powdered milk

2 Tbsp. dehydrated butter or margarine

1/8 tsp. powdered butterscotch flavoring

Honey Butterscotch Candy

Bring 1/2 cup honey to a boil and boil for 1 minute, 15 seconds.
Remove from heat and add 1/2 cup Butterscotch Candy Mix (above).
Add 1/2 cup chopped walnuts (optional). Blend with wire whisk and let
cool in the pan for 1-2 minutes. Pour candy onto a buttered pie plate or
dish. Let cool just long enough to be able to handle it. Butter your
hands and, while candy is still warm, roll to approximately the size of
your little finger and coil it (not touching sides) on a buttered plate. For
a soft candy, cut into 1" pieces and wrap in waxed paper. For hard
candy, cut into bite-sized pieces and dust with powdered sugar. Store in
covered candy dish.

HONEY FRUIT CANDY MIX
Combine:
3 1/3 cups powdered milk
1/2 cup dehydrated butter or margarine
1-2 tsp. orange, lemon or cinnamon powdered flavoring

MINI-MIX
1/3 cup powdered milk
1 Tbsp. dehydrated butter or margarine
1/8 tsp. orange, lemon or cinnamon powdered flavoring

Honey Fruit Candy

Bring 1/2 cup honey to a boil and boil for 1 minute, 15 seconds.
Remove from heat and add 1/2 cup Honey Fruit Candy Mix (above). Add
1/2 cup chopped walnuts (optional). Blend with a wire whisk and let
cool in the pan for 1-2 minutes.

Pour candy onto a buttered pie plate or dish. Let it cool just long
enough to be able to handle it. Butter your hands and, while candy is
still warm, roll to approximately the size of your little finger and coil it
(not touching sides) on the buttered plate.

For a soft candy, cut into 1" pieces and wrap in waxed paper. For hard
candy, cut into bite-sized pieces and dust with powdered sugar. Store in
covered candy dish.

ALPHABETICAL LISTING

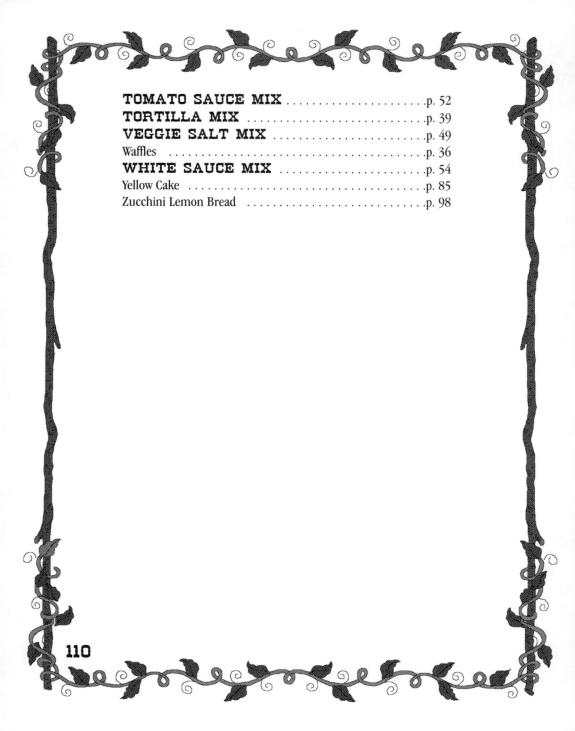

Health Problems?

Need a low-salt diet?
Substitute equal amounts of powdered flavoring for salt in the mixes.
The orange flavoring is wonderful in breads and rolls and the butter-
scotch flavoring is great in cookies.

Problems with refined sugar?
Substitute fructose using only 1/3 to 1/2 as much sugar as is called for
in the mixes.

Weight conscious?
Substitute equal amounts of applesauce for the oil in the recipes.

Wheat allergies?
Try using rice flour in the baking mixes. It works well for muffins and
some cookies, but not for breads.

Notes

Notes

Notes

Notes

Notes

Notes

Notes

Notes

Notes

Notes

Notes

Notes

Mix-A-Meal Company
has a complete line of low-moisture
ingredients and flavorings for making
the fun and easy mixes in
Mix-A-Meal Cookbook

For more information please contact us at:
Mix-A-Meal Company
P.O. Box 971662
Orem, UT 84097-1662
phone 801-221-7465
fax 801-221-7449
info@mixameal.com
http://www.mixameal.com